TRUSTEES OF CULTURE

To Dad — thanks again!

TRUSTEES OF CULTURE
Power, Wealth, and Status on Elite Arts Boards

ç

Francie Ostrower

THE UNIVERSITY OF CHICAGO PRESS

Chicago & London

FRANCIE OSTROWER, Ph.D., is senior research associate in the Center on Nonprofits and Philanthropy at the Urban Institute in Washington, D.C. She is the author of *Why the Wealthy Give: The Culture of Elite Philanthropy,* which won awards from the Association for Research on Nonprofit Organizations and Voluntary Action and Independent Sector, coauthor of *Race, Ethnicity, and Participation in the Arts,* and has also published on various other aspects of philanthropy and arts participation.

THE UNIVERSITY OF CHICAGO PRESS, CHICAGO 60637
THE UNIVERSITY OF CHICAGO PRESS, LTD., LONDON
© 2002 by The University of Chicago
All rights reserved. Published 2002
Printed in the United States of America

11 10 09 08 07 06 05 04 03 02   1 2 3 4 5
ISBN: 0-226-63966-5 (cloth)

Library of Congress Cataloging-in-Publication Data
Ostrower, Francie.
    Trustees of culture : power, wealth, and status on
elite arts boards / Francie Ostrower.
        p.   cm.
    Includes bibliographical references and index.
    ISBN 0-226-63966-5
    1. Arts boards—United States.   2. Arts—United
States—Management   I. Title.
NX765 .O85 2002
700′.68—dc21
                                        2001007373

CONTENTS

Acknowledgments
ix

Introduction
xi

CHAPTER ONE
Elite Trustees: A Profile 1

CHAPTER TWO
*A Dual Approach: Openness and Exclusivity on
the Elite Board* 24

CHAPTER THREE
Diversity and the Elite Board: Race, Ethnicity, and Class 39

CHAPTER FOUR
Fundraising and the Role of the Elite Board 63

CHAPTER FIVE
Status and Governance: A Delicate Balance 85

CHAPTER SIX
Conclusion 107

CONTENTS

Notes 115
Bibliography 125
Index 131

ACKNOWLEDGMENTS

MY SINCEREST THANKS to Paul J. DiMaggio and Stanley Katz for support and thoughtful comments and suggestions at various points in this research. For providing financial assistance that was invaluable in launching and carrying out this study, I am grateful to the Lilly Endowment and the Yale University Program on Non-Profit Organizations (PONPO), and to Peter Dobkin Hall, then of PONPO, for his support of this work. I am thankful as well for generous financial assistance received from the Aspen Institute's Nonprofit Sector Research Fund. As a faculty member at Harvard University during this project, I received a university-supported leave of absence that was most helpful in bringing this project to completion, and for that I am grateful.

I wish to extend very deeply felt thanks to the trustees and staff members who took time from busy schedules to speak with me; without their assistance this project would not have been possible. Their willingness to speak in such depth and to share their thoughts and observations made the process of conducting this study both interesting and enjoyable.

My thanks as well to the many individuals, too numerous to name, who have shared comments and questions, at talks or in discussions, over the course of this research.

INTRODUCTION

THIS BOOK SHOWS how power, wealth, and status come together as central elements in the functioning of the elite boards of four major arts institutions in two large American cities. These institutions, two opera companies and two museums, are themselves elite by virtue of their size and wealth, and their trustees are largely drawn from social and economic elites. To quote one trustee, these boards are indeed "high-powered" places. This book explores the roles played by these boards for both their organizations and the elite. In the process, it shows that elite boards are cultural entities as well as governance bodies. It also shows that, as such, these boards function within a delicate, and sometimes precarious, balance between class-based influences and the dictates of the large-scale organizations that they oversee.

Material from personal interviews I conducted with 76 board members provides the foundation for this book. These trustees are referred to as "elite" in this book primarily because of their wealth. Many are also elite by virtue of other criteria, such as occupation and social status. They own and/or run companies, are listed in society bluebooks, belong to exclusive clubs, and have important political connections. As trustees put it, these boards include "movers and shakers in the region," who get their "phone calls returned." By virtue of their overall elite status, these trustees bring considerable economic, social, and political resources to the institutions that they oversee. In many ways, these boards face challenges and assume roles common to boards more generally. They approach and implement those roles, however, in ways that are deeply shaped by their class.

Interviews with these trustees provide otherwise inaccessible information on the highly private world of elite boards, and on the motivations, outlooks, and activities of their members. These interviews provide the base, but the book also incorporates additional data that I compiled from organizational and archival sources, such as annual reports, and material from supplemental interviews with other relevant parties, such as professional staff. To provide a wider context, the discussion also draws at points on 99 personal interviews with donors and trustees of other nonprofit institutions interviewed for my earlier book on elite philanthropy.[1]

The present study grew out of that earlier work on philanthropy, which underscored the close links between trusteeship and major giving, and highlighted the class-related motivations and prestige associated with board service. Indeed, one donor went so far as to wryly characterize board membership as a virtually mandatory "accoutrement" of wealth. That study explored the significance of trusteeship for elite philanthropy but also raised a question that it could not answer: Do the meanings and motivations that affluent donors associate with trusteeship influence how they actually think and behave as trustees? That is the question that this study set out to address. The answer that I found was that the class-related influences do indeed shape the boards' approach, but in a complex way that is mediated by organizational influences and constraints. Elite arts boards, in short, must be understood in relation to the dual, and often conflicting, influences of class and organization.

This introduction presents the basic approach, perspective, and context of this book, including both its goals and boundaries. Boards are complex entities that can be studied from multiple perspectives. This book, accordingly, is not intended as an exhaustive treatment of boards—even of the four boards included in the study. Rather, it addresses a specific set of issues about elite arts boards and offers one particular thesis that, I believe, explains a good deal about how their members think and act across a variety of areas. That includes the boards' seemingly contradictory behavior at times and their response to major contemporary challenges such as expanding audiences and increasing diversity. Therefore, this book will range across many aspects of board culture, structure, and functioning, but it will do so in a delimited way that relates to its particular focus and perspective.

Elite Arts Boards and Their Significance

Elite arts boards are relevant to our understanding of organizational governance, cultural philanthropy, and arts participation. They are also, I contend, of central importance to our understanding of arts policy. Boards do not exist in a vacuum. Rather, the way that they function reflects a wider system that has developed out of the emphasis on *private* support and governance of arts institutions in the United States.[2] Examining elite arts boards, accordingly, helps to illuminate the consequences of this system and to identify both its characteristic capabilities and limitations.

Within this system, the wealthy have been an essential source of support for the arts, and the study of arts boards contributes to our understanding of their patronage. Elites have been integral to founding, sustaining, and overseeing arts institutions in many cities.[3] This is certainly true of the institutions in this study, including both one city's older, nineteenth-century institutions, as well as the newer institutions of the other city, founded in the twentieth century. All four of the opera companies and museums would be radically different without elite support, if they continued to exist at all.

Elites have influenced these institutions not only through the money that they provide, but through the values and goals that they support as donors and trustees. These large and complex institutions are run by professional managers, including arts administrators who demand authority over artistic matters on the basis of their expertise. That professional authority, however, is exercised within parameters set by the board, which hires and fires the organization's director. At these organizations, those parameters are determined by the boards' commitment to a particular vision of artistic and institutional excellence. As we shall see, these boards can and do assert themselves when they believe their fundamental goals are at stake or their authority is being challenged. Those who seek to understand arts institutions and/or implement managerial or artistic policies through them must ultimately deal with the board because of its authority.

Elites have been important for arts institutions, but the institutions have also played a status-related role for elite patrons that goes beyond their aesthetic function. Accordingly, the study of boards can also contribute to our understanding of elite status processes and the links between arts participation and wider elite values and identity. Particularly, as the bases of elite status have shifted from family and community to formal organizations,[4] the study of boards helps to illuminate the centrality of organizations to the social and cultural life of contemporary elites.

Most of the literature on nonprofit boards in general is managerial or prescriptive in orientation.[5] Far less is available on how boards actually do behave and why, and no comparable book exists on elite boards or boards of arts institutions. A central purpose of this book, accordingly, is to help fill a gap in the existing literature on elites, arts institutions, and nonprofit boards. Although this book is not a study in management, its findings are relevant to managerial concerns. This book seeks to understand boards, a task that is critical for those who work with and through arts institutions, as well as those who study them. Throughout the book, for instance, we shall see the very different outcomes that ensue depending on whether or not professional staff understand the perspective of their boards, which may be very different from their own.

In general, more research is available on the numerical presence of elites on the boards of large, wealthy nonprofits than are studies that investigate what elites actually think and do as trustees. Evidence also suggests that shifts have been occurring in the composition of elite boards.[6] The qualitative and interview-based approach taken in this study also helps to clarify the meaning and significance of quantitative trends that have been noted in the literature. This book contributes to our understanding of what significance board composition, and shifts in that composition, have for how trustees carry out their roles.

Although this book contributes to the literature on a number of fronts, the limitations must again be emphasized. As has been observed by both myself and others, boards are a heterogeneous group, and much additional work is needed on boards of all sizes and types to fill the gaps in our current knowledge.

The Thesis: Class, Organization, and the Dual Approach of Elite Boards

The purpose of this book is to present, develop, and apply a particular thesis on elite arts boards that takes into account the dual influences of class and organization. That thesis, concerning the existence and impact of a bifurcation in trustee outlook, is summarized here by way of introduction. In future chapters, it will be developed and applied to various areas of board culture, structure, and operations.

Elite boards are subject to two major, but often conflicting influences. One is rooted in trustees' class background, and the other is based in the organizational needs of the large, complex institutions that they govern. The affluent men and women who serve on these arts boards attach class-based prestige and meaning to them and to involvement with art and arts institutions. These class-related values attract affluent people to boards and encourage large donations. As actual board members, elites do not abandon their class-based outlook. At the same time, however, organizational pressures and considerations come into play. Sometimes, class and organizational influences push in similar directions. Often, however, they are in tension. While class-based influences promote exclusivity and traditionalism, organizational needs often call for greater openness and change. Accordingly elites adapt.

In response to the dual influences of class and organization, I contend, elites develop a bifurcation in their own outlook and actions. When it comes to organizational accessibility and operations, contemporary trustees think and act in ways that are often surprisingly at odds with traditional stereotypes of elite exclusivity. At the same time, however, other trustee attitudes perpetuate the board itself as an exclusive elite enclave. In short, elite boards respond to the dual influences of class and organization by functioning on two related but distinct tracks.

Theorists have debated whether organizations should be viewed as instruments of cohesive upper classes that control them (e.g., as members of their boards), or whether class influences have been eclipsed by the imperatives of large-scale, formal organization.[7] At least with respect to elite arts boards, this book contends, both come into play and must be taken into account not only by researchers, but by trustees themselves. With respect to elite theory, therefore, this book's findings indicate the limitations of a class control perspective for understanding elite boards.[8]

Class and the Perspective of Trustees

Trustees serve on these elite boards for multiple reasons.[9] Many have an interest, sometimes a passionate one, in the mission of the institution. For instance, one opera trustee serves because, "I always loved the opera, all my life, since I was a child." He explained that his position on the board gives him the chance, as someone who is not an artist, to be a part of the institution, and represents the "fulfillment of a lifelong dream." Board membership is also valued as a way to support the community, and many enjoy the interaction with fellow trustees. For many affluent women volunteering represents a worthwhile and interesting alternative to paid work. Many affluent men who do work enjoy the involvement in an activity outside of their business life.

These affluent men and women, however, also attach class-based meanings to trusteeship and to involvement with arts institutions. These class-related values enhance the desirability of board service and encourage large donations from trustees. Indeed, board prestige is something that trustees and professional staff quite consciously cultivate.[10] As one said, the "social cachet" of the board is "something we have to be aware of, and have also to use." So desirable is a board seat that some donors will exert considerable effort to gain one, including donations of considerable sums of money. Many trustees simply take a link between trusteeship and their philanthropic giving for granted. Thus, when asked whether they would contribute as much money were they not on the board, some trustees simply said that would not be possible—because then they would be members of another board, and so would be giving the money to those institutions. This outlook also reflects the sense of involvement and identification with the institutions that is developed and valued by trustees.

As this suggests, and central to this book's approach, it is critical to distinguish between an interest in art and an involvement with the formal organizations that produce art. Although the two are related, they are not the same. This distinction is important to an appreciation of the multiplicity of aesthetic and nonaesthetic reasons why elites get involved with the arts, as well as the particular ways in which they become involved.

The distinction was brought home, albeit in an atypically dramatic way during an interview I conducted for a previous study[11] with a trustee of a modern art museum. As it turned out, this trustee, also a large donor, actually disliked modern art, or, as he characterized it, "people with four eyes and six arms." He explained that he had felt pressured to become a trustee by a friend, who was the head of the board. Certainly, most arts trustees do not dislike art, and in that respect this man was atypical. What is typical is the fact that nonaesthetic considerations drew him to the board. Such considerations have an influence even among those who do appreciate the artistic work of their institutions, a point illustrated by the case of another modern art museum trustee. This man loves art but also acknowledged that "social snobbery" played a role in his decision to become a trustee. He was, he said, "thrilled" when invited to join this prestigious board.

The opera company and museum trustees in this study also bring a multiplicity of motives, both aesthetic and nonaesthetic to their roles. And, as is also central to this book's perspective, it is critical to recognize and analyze those reasons, for the motives that bring them to the board also influence how elites think and act as trustees.

The Trustees, the Organizations, and the Cities

Personal interviews with 76 trustees of four arts institutions in two large American cities form the primary basis of this study. Between 40 and 56 percent of the members of each board were interviewed.[12] All board chairs and presidents were interviewed. The trustees spoke at length, and interviews averaged one hour and 40 minutes in length (the median was just over one and a half hours), and ranged from 40 minutes to three and a half hours. The elite composition of these boards is so central to this book that it is the subject of the entire first chapter, where a detailed description of trustees (including both interviewees and noninterviewees) is presented.

One of the first decisions I had to make was whether to include smaller numbers of trustees from many different boards or to interview many trustees from fewer boards. While both approaches have advantages and disadvantages, for the specific purposes of this research, the advantages of focusing on trustees from the same boards proved decisive. As interviews repeatedly confirmed, individual trustee roles vary in terms of intensity and area (e.g., an interviewee knowledgeable about board recruitment processes might have little familiarity with the finance committee).[13] Interviewing multiple trustees from the same board, therefore, proved critical in gaining an understanding not only of individual motivations and activities but of the overall nature and functioning of the elite board as a distinct entity.

In one sense, organizations were selected for this study on the basis of their similarities. All four are among the largest and wealthiest arts institutions in their cities and in the country. To underscore the elite stature of the institutions, it is useful to place them within the larger context of the arts field. The world of arts organizations is a highly stratified one, in which a relatively small number of large institutions receive the bulk of resources. According to one estimate, fewer than 10 percent of arts organizations have annual expenses in excess of one million dollars, yet these same institutions receive over 75 percent of all public support.[14] The arts organizations in this study belong to that small group. Their prominence attracts affluent men and women to the board, and trustees' commitment to maintaining institutional size and stature is reflected in the approach taken by their boards. Thus, the study intentionally did not seek out boards of "typical" arts institutions, but rather focused on elite organizations. In addition to the size and stature of the institutions and the composition of their boards, the focus on arts boards must be kept in mind. Neither boards nor philanthropy are homogeneous, and area of activity is one important source of variation. Comparative evidence suggests that large fine arts boards are more elite in composition,[15] and even among elites, motivations for different types of philanthropic involvements also vary (although there are important overlaps as well).[16]

A question that naturally arises, however, is the extent to which trustees of these four boards may or may not even resemble trustees of comparable institutions. While this question cannot be answered definitively without a random sample of such trustees, available evidence does at least indicate that they are not atypical or drawn from a separate and unique pool. That conclusion is suggested by trustees' wider patterns of board membership. Although they were interviewed because of their affiliations with the four boards in this study, the vast majority of trustees on all four boards (from 76 to 92.9 percent) also served on other boards. Those who did served on an average of 3.22 other boards.[17] Indeed, many trustees also served together on boards other than the four included in this research.[18]

A consideration of the types of other boards on which they served particularly suggests a wider involvement and concentration in the arts, but one that also coexists with other types of institutional involvements. Among those who serve on other boards, more served on other arts boards (65.7 percent) than served on boards in any other single area. At the same time, the vast majority (83.2 percent) did sit on the board of some type of organization other than arts, usually in higher education (38 percent) or health, generally hospitals (31.9 percent).[19] By contrast, very few trustees (11.1 percent) sat on the board of a social service institution. In short, the involvements of these trustees conform to patterns of elite philanthropy more generally[20] and indicate that the trustees in this study are likely typical of, and involved with, arts boards more generally in their community. It also suggests, however, that the social services and the arts, at least in these cities, are drawing their trustees from rather different pools. An important area for future research would be to consider what, if any, implications this has for the character of boards in these different areas.

While the four institutions were deliberately intended to be similar with respect to their elite stature and area of activity, differences were also deliberately introduced. Thus, different types of arts institutions (two operas and two museums), from two different cities were included for study. Opera companies are performing arts institutions, unlike museums, which are in the visual arts. The two museums in this study, like many others, have longstanding and important ties with local government, an important source of financial resources. The two opera companies, by contrast, receive little funding from government at any level and rely almost exclusively on earned income and private donations. Moreover, by comparison with other institutions traditionally classified as "high cultural," opera companies and museums fall at different ends of the spectrum with respect to the elite character of their audience. Opera draws its audience from the smallest, and art museums from the largest, percentage of the population.[21] Similarly, the audience for opera is most, and the audience for art museums least, concentrated among those in the highest socioeconomic category.[22]

In addition to selecting different types of arts institutions, I chose institutions from two different cities. Within each city, the boards of the largest opera company and art museum (as measured by annual expenditures) were selected for study. Both of the museums are encyclopedic and general in nature, rather than focused on a specific type of art. In order to preserve respondent confidentiality, the two cities will be referred to as Orchid City and Tulip City. The two cities are comparable in that both are large, ethnically diverse, and home to large numbers of affluent individuals. They are, however, located in different (and geographically distant) regions of the country and have different traditions of cultural philanthropy.

Orchid City is the older city and has older, more extensive, and more established traditions of cultural philanthropy. This is reflected in the ages of the two city's arts institutions. While the Orchid City museum and opera were established by nineteenth-century elites, Tulip City's institutions are products of the twentieth century. Indeed, for Tulip City trustees, remedying the city's historical dearth of major arts institutions was taken as a matter of civic pride, viewed as necessary to joining the ranks of "world-class" cities. Orchid City trustees, by contrast, are confident in the "world-class" status of both their city and its arts institutions.

I went to study the boards of these institutions with such differences in mind. Yet as the research progressed, I was increasingly struck by the strong similarities that cut across all four, and that is reflected in the emphasis of this book. It was not only that the trustees and the boards share many outward similarities, although that is the case. It was also that, as I argue, all four boards exhibit a similar underlying dynamic and approach that influences how they appear and function across a variety of areas. A central insight of elite theory is that elites and their institutions must adapt if they are to survive.[23] In this book, I extend that insight to show how elite trustees adapt in ways that preserve their unique relationship with these institutions even as they recognize the reality and necessity of organizational change.

Many of the largest and most affluent arts institutions, such as those in this study, find themselves today in cities that have been changing dramatically since they were first established. The magnitude of the resources involved and pressing issues concerning the place of such organizations in a changing, diverse, and multicultural urban environment makes the governance of these institutions (and the role of the board in shaping the organization's relationship to the larger community) an issue of vital concern. This book sheds light on whether, when, and how, elite trustees and donors are willing to respond to environmental pressures for change, and how little or much change they might be willing to accept before withdrawing their financial support.

This book draws on a rich set of data, but conclusions based on these data cannot automatically be generalized to other boards and cities. There is, however, good reason to believe that the findings of this book are more widely applicable. I found commonalities among elite arts boards located in different parts of the country, and in cities with different traditions of cultural philanthropy. We also have ample evidence of elite involvement with arts organizations in many American cities.[24] Still, future research is needed to establish just how widely this book's conclusions may be applied, as well as what important differences may exist among other boards and cities.

Overview of the Book

This book develops and applies its thesis concerning elite arts boards across diverse aspects of board culture, structure, and operations. Chapter 1 presents a profile of trustees and establishes their elite status. It shows how the elite status of the board is maintained, even as board composition and recruitment also adapts to shifting organizational and environmental circumstances. Chapter 2 elaborates on this book's thesis concerning the bifurcation in trustees' outlook and activities. In doing so, it presents the dual patterns of openness (with respect to organizational functioning and services) and exclusivity (with respect to the board) exhibited by trustees. Chapter 3 examines issues surrounding ethnic and racial diversity from within the book's perspective, addressing the relationship between ethnic, racial, and class homogeneity and heterogeneity. Chapter 4 applies the book's perspective to how trustees define, prioritize, and implement their roles. Particular attention is given to fundraising, a role that is very strongly emphasized by these boards. It also shows how gender works, in relation to class, to influence how trustees carry out their roles. Chapter 5 explores the distinctive culture of excellence that informs trustees' approach to the board and these institutions. Building on themes developed throughout the book, the chapter highlights the ongoing, inherent tensions rooted in the board's status-related dimensions and its character as a governance body. The final chapter concludes by considering further implications of the book's perspective and analysis.

CHAPTER ONE

Elite Trustees:
A Profile

A central theme of this book is that there is a duality in trustees' outlook and activities. Although trustees display a sometimes surprising openness concerning organizational accessibility and services, their approach perpetuates the nature of the board itself as an exclusive elite enclave. This chapter shows that these boards are indeed elite in their composition. As one trustee said of his opera board, "it doesn't have a lot of ordinary people." As a multimillionaire himself, this man exemplifies his own point, and his observation applies to all the boards in this study.

The composition of the boards is closely connected to the way in which they recruit new members. Boards are self-perpetuating entities. New members are selected by current trustees, who typically look to other members of their class. This is not to say that trustees overtly focus on class exclusivity, or that they are unconcerned with the needs of the institution. Boards take the recruitment process seriously, and the nominating committee is among the most important of board committees. As trustees emphasize, prospective members are assessed in relation to their ability to contribute to the board and the institution. Yet the very criteria used in this evaluation, and the ways that potential candidates are identified inherently favor members of the elite.

Although organizational considerations reinforce class-based recruitment criteria in certain respects, they have also become a source of tension. As the institutions, their circumstances, and the elite change, boards adapt their recruitment strategies and criteria. Yet such adaptations typically result in expanding or altering the types of elites recruited or the types of elite resources (e.g., wealth versus social connections) emphasized—but not in crossing class lines. Board composition changes, but it remains exclusive with respect to class.

Class sets the basic framework for understanding board composition, but race and gender are also important, and often operate in relation to class. Trustees are overwhelmingly white men and women of European descent, a fact that bears on organizational legitimacy, survival, and relations with the wider community. As we shall see in a future chapter, ethnic and racial diversity is a major issue for these boards, and one that they approach in ways that are shaped by class.

Considerably more heterogeneity exists with respect to gender, but traditional upper-class gender divisions are reflected in the types of men and women recruited, and the roles that they assume on boards. Trustees say that gender diversity, as opposed to racial and ethnic diversity, is not an issue because of the greater numerical presence of women on their boards. As women increasingly move into higher positions in business, from which so many male trustees are drawn, however, it will be of major interest to follow possible shifts in the *types* of women recruited, and the potential consequences for boards.

Elite Trustees and Publicity: A Note on Data

The vast majority of material in this book is not publicly available and could be obtained only through personal interviews with trustees. Considerable data on board composition, however, can be compiled from published sources. The public availability of such material permits the expansion of this chapter's analysis beyond interviewees, to include all board members for whom information was found.[1]

The availability of published information about trustees has substantive as well as methodological relevance and is indicative of the elite composition of the boards. Some trustees were found on national and/or regional lists of wealthy individuals, such as the *Forbes* 400. Some attracted media coverage because they own distinguished art collections, are major philanthropic donors, or are large political contributors. Some received media attention because of their extensive business holdings, involvement in major financial transactions (such as the sale, acquisition, or merger of a company), and prominent business position. Salaries of some trustees are published in corporate proxy statements because they are top executives in public companies. Some trustees are listed in society bluebooks. The prominence of many is reflected in their inclusion in *Who's Who* volumes, with biographical entries that list a myriad of business, social, and political affiliations.

Affluence and the Elite Board

All four of these boards' trustees are drawn overwhelmingly from the ranks of the affluent. Indeed, one trustee characterized fellow board members as a varied group because, "there are people of vast wealth, and people of just wealth, you know." Virtually every trustee (96 percent) was a millionaire. The percentage of millionaires on individual boards ranged from 94 to 100 percent.[2] Most trustees were multimillionaires (between 76 and 96 percent).[3] In this environment, annual *incomes* in excess of a

3

million dollars are not uncommon and were earned by over half of trustees.[4] Indeed, a trustee whose earnings are in the mid-six figures actually declined to join his board at first because he felt his resources were inadequate and would not permit him to make donations comparable to those made by many other members. He was ultimately convinced to join on the basis that he raises enormous sums of money.

Both of the opera companies have associated support organizations, and a comparison of their boards underscores the significance of affluence on the main opera boards. Thus, a Tulip Opera trustee explained that at their support institution "you can contribute to the opera without having a lot of money." An Orchid Opera trustee said that while the opera includes people because they can make very large donations, on the support organization board, "people are there because they work." There is overlap among trustees of the operas and their support institutions, and the boards of the latter also include some very wealthy people. As one trustee said, however, the difference is that "they are not there because they're rich. They're there because they can play some role."

These boards do include individuals who are less wealthy, but they are seen as exceptions, both by themselves and by other trustees. Their experiences on the board highlight trustees' more typical affluence. For instance, one museum trustee, who is *not* a millionaire, said that it does get "embarrassing" at board-related dinners when people ask whether he and his wife are collectors. Anecdotes and comments of this nature convey perhaps more than statistical percentages, because they show how deeply the culture of these boards is built around wealth. So, too, does the self-consciousness expressed by other less affluent trustees about their inability to make donations comparable to those of many peers, regardless of their other forms of participation on the board.

Among trustees who are not taken on as exceptions, failure to contribute can result in being asked to leave the board. A woman I initially contacted for an interview declined and said that she was no longer a member. She explained that because of the family's financial difficulties, "we couldn't face the demands" for donations. Although saddened to leave, she said she cannot criticize the board's financial criteria, because donations are "a big necessity."In this context, we can well understand a comment made by another trustee who was able to underwrite an opera after coming into some money. Said she, "That was very nice, and in a funny way, that gave us credibility in a world where money matters."

Occupations among Male and Female Trustees

Consistent with their economic resources, business was the predominant occupation among board members. The majority of employed trustees on all four boards were in business and financial positions.[5] But not all trustees did work, and whether or not they did is closely related to gender. The occupational profiles of male and female trustees are quite distinct, and reflect traditional gender divisions in the elite.

Most of the male board members worked (86 percent), and all of the other men were retired from former careers. Among those at work, the great majority (70 percent) were in business or finance, followed by 15 percent in law, with the balance in other professional and managerial positions. Moreover, these men do not only work in business institutions—they typically own and/or run them, serving as chairs, presidents, and CEOs.[6]

Traditionally, upper-class women have not occupied the

positions of economic and social authority held by their male counterparts,[7] and this is reflected in trustees' occupational status. In contrast to men, fewer than one fifth of women on these boards worked, and only another 16 percent were retirees. Among the few women active in a career, most (56 percent) also worked in business or finance, with the remainder divided among other managerial and professional positions. These businesswomen also held senior positions, virtually all in businesses owned personally or by their families.

To the extent that women increasingly reach prominent positions in business, women with business careers will also be more likely to appear on these boards. Given that gender-related occupational differences do influence board roles, a major question is whether, as trustees, businesswomen will assume traditional roles of female trustees, or whether their activities will more closely resemble those of businessmen on boards. It is a question to which we return in chapter 4, when we consider trustee roles.

The prevalence of businesspeople on these boards illustrates how board composition responds to organizational needs as defined and addressed by these elite boards. The presence of many businesspeople on these boards reflects their personal wealth, but businesspeople are also seen as providing essential financial skills. Indeed, these boards do include some businesspeople who are not very wealthy (by their standards) because of their business skills. As one trustee explained, "You need businesspeople for a lot of things like [the] investment committee." Others similarly said that businesspeople have the specialized technical expertise needed for various finance-related committees.

Organizational developments also enhance the value that boards placed on business experience. As these museums and operas have grown, become more complex, and increasingly engaged in retail and marketing activities, their boards have felt the need to recruit members with expertise in these areas. Some businesspeople, for instance, were brought onto the board precisely because the institution had initiated, or planned to initiate, new levels of commercial activity.

Elite boards are not unique in addressing financial matters, and various types of boards have finance-related committees. When elite boards recruit trustees to assume financial oversight roles, however, they do so in a way that reflects their elite status. Specifically, they recruit those at the very top of the business world, who also fit within the board's general culture of affluence. Moreover, these boards try to recruit those who bring both financial skills and financial resources. Thus, while acknowledging the importance of business skills, one nominating committee member cautioned that skills alone are generally not sufficient in a potential candidate because "You want marketable skills, but you also either want a financial contribution and/or the ability to raise money."

The Art Collection as an Elite Resource

Museum and opera boards both draw on those with considerable resources. In the case of museums, however, a distinguished art collection is a uniquely important resource. Collectors are a strong presence at both museums, comprising just under 40 percent of the Orchid Museum, and just over 40 percent of the Tulip Museum boards. Most had loaned, donated, or promised works of art to the museums. Indeed, an interest in their collection is one reason they are recruited by these boards. The fact that so many trustees own collections desired by major museums is yet a further illustration of the board's elite composition.

A member of one museum's nominating committee succinctly explained why so many collectors are recruited to the board: "Obviously, [the museum] has them there for their knowledge, and in the hope of getting their collection." Collectors realize that this contributes to their desirability as trustees. Explaining his longevity on the museum board, one active and influential trustee said, "They don't want to lose me, and they don't want to lose the collection." One collector made a board seat a condition of making a donation. She was given the seat and donated a gallery. As this shows, museums value collectors, but collectors also seek an association with these prestigious institutions and their boards.

The mere presence of a collector on the board, however, does not guarantee that their collection or the particular pieces desired will actually go to the museum. Considerable time may elapse before trustees confirm that they will permanently donate a work of art that they have loaned or decide how much of their collection will be donated to the organization. And, sometimes, collectors change their minds. In some cases, the collector's position as donor and trustee are mutually reinforcing, but in other cases a collector's agenda as a donor has resulted in tension, and even open conflict with the rest of the board and the institution. Both museums have had collectors who eventually left the board following such conflicts. The negotiations and intrigue, as well as the excitement surrounding donations of major pieces by collectors shapes the culture, as well as the composition, of museum boards. One trustee, for instance, enjoys her involvement at the museum more than other board memberships because, "They need huge amounts of money, but you also come in contact with people who have a passion that doesn't have anything to do with money. So you are with passionate people who have enormous knowledge, and can contribute by giving their collections."

Others spoke of the value of including collectors on the board because of their suitability for service on the acquisitions committee and their familiarity with art or a particular art form. Yet knowledge of art per se is not considered a prerequisite for board membership, and these institutions do not seek out those with great enthusiasm and knowledge who lack comparable financial resources. Rather, when these boards speak of recruiting people who are involved with art, they typically mean those who have valuable collections or the resources to help acquire art. In short, they look to members of the elite.

Political Connections as an Elite Resource

Political connections are another resource that trustees bring to these boards. While opera and museum boards both include individuals who have such connections by virtue of their elite position, at museums it is an attribute that figures explicitly in recruiting trustees. Although far less prominent than in the case of collectors, the importance of political connections is thus another area of contrast between museums and operas. The difference reflects the museums' closer relationship with local city government, an important source of revenue for both museums, but for neither opera.

Political access is far less pervasive than wealth or art collections as a consideration in board recruitment, and most trustees are not involved in organizational dealings with government.

Yet it does still represent an important resource, and one that is considered by nominating committees. For instance, a Tulip Museum nominating committee explained, "we should always have some people who are politically involved—at least on a local level." Thus, although he rarely attends meetings, a member of this board is considered important, because he makes large annual gifts and has political connections. As a fellow trustee put it, "like it or not, we're involved in politics all the time."

Asked whether government ties were a factor in recruiting trustees at the Orchid Museum, a nominating committee member said, "Yes, very definitely," and went on to explain: "We need, hopefully, to get people who understand the importance of the public dimension, and have relationships through their work with the leadership of the city, including the Mayor. We don't pick them just for that reason, but having that's a plus." Trustees with such connections can help get a hearing for the institution's point of view from politicians and can rally support among other influential members of the community. Issues on which trustees have undertaken such efforts range from responding to proposed cuts in government funding for arts institutions, to relevant tax and public transportation issues.

When it comes to incorporating those with political access, these boards once again turn to members of the economic and social elite. As one trustee put it, such people have political access because of their "standing in other areas." As the head of a major business who has political connections, he is an example. He explained that when it comes to assisting in the museum's relationship with government, "Mostly what you do is you use the access you have, and the relationships you have developed in other venues, but you use those for the benefit of this organization."[8]

Race, Ethnicity, and the Elite Board

The vast majority of trustees are non-Hispanic white men and women of European descent, who constitute 90 percent or more of each board. The balance are trustees of Hispanic and African-American descent.[9] Asians and Asian-Americans have served on these boards, in some cases recently, but none were serving at the time of the interviews. The ethnic and racial composition of Tulip and Orchid City boards is in sharp contrast to their diverse cities, where whites of non-Hispanic origin comprise less than half of the population.

As with white trustees, virtually all of the Hispanic and African-American men and women on these boards were millionaires.[10] As this suggests, when these boards try to introduce diversity with respect to ethnicity and race, as they all say they want to do, they do so in ways that remain within the boundaries of class. The subject is given extended treatment in chapter 3.

Gender

Although most trustees (64 percent) were men, all four boards are far more diverse with respect to gender than race. Women accounted for 40–45 percent of the two Orchid City boards, and 30–35 percent of the Tulip City boards.[11] As occupational profiles highlight, most of these women are in traditional upper-class female roles. Most of them do not work in a paid career. Philanthropic involvements, which are quite extensive for many, have long offered a socially acceptable and rewarding role outside of the home for affluent women. Indeed, women have a far stronger presence on these arts boards than they do on corporate boards,[12] consistent with the greater opportunities women have historically found for public and leadership roles in volunteer activities.[13] As noted, gender does have a bearing on trustee roles, to be explored in chapter 4.

At museums, there is also a distinctive gender-related route onto the board for some women, who assume board seats vacated by a husband, a practice reminiscent of "widow's succession" in politics. Fully 39 percent of the women on the Tulip Museum board, and over one fifth of those at the Orchid Museum were preceded on the board by their husbands. By contrast, a husband followed a wife onto a board in only one case, and they were opera trustees. In the case of museums, women assumed a board seat after a husband died, became ill, or reached one board's mandatory retirement age. This last case also illustrates that even policies that formally promote turnover (i.e., mandatory retirement) can be consistent with continued insularity, depending on how they are implemented in practice.

This was not a recruitment strategy mentioned by trustees themselves, who may not even realize how often it occurs, but one that became evident from reviewing past lists of trustees. The particular cases in which wives were appointed, suggests that one factor at work was the museum's desire to retain a relationship to important collectors. This explanation is consistent with the fact that the pattern is common at museums but is not found at the operas.

The Religious Composition of the Boards

Protestants (primarily Episcopalians) constituted the largest single religious group (42 percent) among trustees and on three of the boards, but were a majority only on the two Orchid City boards. A considerable percentage of board members were

Jewish (30 percent), and Catholics comprised just under 18 percent.[14] The others either had another or, in most cases, no religious affiliation.

The considerable presence of Jewish trustees is noteworthy because of historical barriers against Jewish participation in the Protestant-dominated social elite and related institutions, including prestigious arts boards. Trustees in both cities were well aware that religion had been a source of differentiation and exclusion. Jews and non-Jews alike said this was no longer the case, and indeed the figures show that many Jews do serve on these boards. We shall return to this issue at the end of the chapter as part of a consideration of shifting board composition.

Family, Inheritance, and Social Origins of Elite Trustees

All four boards are comprised primarily of elites, but differ in the extent to which their members were born into affluent and socially prominent families. Consistent with the older and more established character of the city and its elite, a greater percentage of Orchid City trustees were millionaires by virtue of inheritance. The Orchid Museum board stands out most sharply in the extent to which it includes descendants of elite families. Here alone did inheritors comprise over half of the board, a figure that falls to just over one-third at the Orchid Opera, under 20 percent at the Tulip Museum, and under 10 percent at the Tulip Opera.[15]

The Orchid Museum also consistently ranks highest on all measures of elite social origins. Parents of more than half the museums's trustees had been listed in a society bluebook, a figure that drops to 25 percent at the Orchid Opera, and is between 15 and 20 percent at the Tulip City organizations. Parents of fully 80 percent of Orchid Museum trustees belonged to one or more clubs, a figure that drops to 45 percent at the Orchid Opera, 42 percent at the Tulip Opera, and under 15 percent at the Tulip Museum.[16] Almost 80 percent of Orchid Museum trustees' parents served on philanthropic boards, as did 57 percent of Orchid Opera trustees' parents, as compared with one-third and under at the Tulip City institutions.

An additional indicator of upper-class origins is attendance at prestigious prep schools.[17] Again, the percentage of graduates is highest at the Orchid Museum (one-third), followed by the Orchid Opera (one-fourth). The figure is under 10 percent at the Tulip City institutions, but this indicator is also less appropriate for Tulip City, whose affluent families have not generally sent children to these institutions. The difference between the cities is meaningful, however, in conveying again the more established nature of Orchid City elites and their association with exclusive institutions.

In some cases, trustees not only came from families with prestigious social affiliations but had been preceded by a family member on this same arts board.[18] When asked how he first came to join the Orchid Museum board, for instance, one such individual replied, "very bluntly, because of my family background." Previous family links existed among 14 percent of Orchid Museum trustees, 10 percent of Orchid Opera board members, and under 5 percent at the Tulip City organizations (whose more recent founding also makes this less likely). At the Orchid Museum, though, family links have a greater salience than suggested by the 14 percent figure, because those with such links are among the board's most influential members. They include all the board officers, half of the nominating committee, and over one-third of the executive committee.

Today, however, none of these four boards can be understood as the domain of a small group of "old" families. Indeed, even the Orchid Museum board, which most closely conforms to the image of an upper-class arts board, has changed and adapted to incorporate different types of elite members. In doing so, it has brought them together in ways that bring the institution new sources of support and that bolster and perpetuate the prestige and influence of the board over time.

When we turn from parents' affiliations to trustees' own, current social affiliations, a far more similar picture emerges. Thus, the percent of trustees listed in a society bluebook ranged only from 27 percent to 31 percent among the boards. At three organizations, the percent of members belonging to an exclusive social club ranged from 40 to just over 51 percent (at the fourth, the Tulip Museum, less than 15 percent belonged).

For an overview, it is useful to employ a combined measure of social elite membership, developed by sociologist G. William Domhoff (1983). With this approach, someone is classified as a member of the social elite if they belong to an exclusive club, or graduated from a prestigious prep school, or appear in a society bluebook. By that indicator, the percentage of those belonging to the social elite ranged from a low of 43 percent (at the Tulip Museum) to a high of 63 percent (at the Orchid Museum). Such figures are indicative of the prestigious social connections that trustees bring to the boards.

Recruitment Strategies and
the Elite Composition of the Board

The elite composition of the board is perpetuated both directly and indirectly by the way in which new trustees are recruited. Boards select their own members, and when they do, they typically turn to others of their class. Trustees think of those who are known to them through their social and business networks. This does not mean that they suggest their close friends, but they do suggest those who move within similar worlds. As one museum trustee put it, when the nominating committee asks for suggestions, "what you recommend is your own kind."

Consider the following examples from an opera board. One trustee's involvement with the opera began when a friend (who became a trustee) convinced him to attend a performance. He enjoyed it, became a large contributor, and joined the board. Once on the board, he proposed a candidate for membership, someone he knew from business, "who could give good sums of money, and was a nice person . . . A good, broad-guaged person who was head of his own company."

This example illustrates how networks used to recruit trustees contribute to perpetuating class homogeneity on the board. It further illustrates that the very criteria trustees use to define a good board member favor those with considerable resources, particularly economic resources. For instance, the trustee just described was not proposing his business associate for the board simply because he liked him, but because he had financial skills and could "give good sums of money." Given the centrality accorded to the fundraising role of the board, having wealth or access to wealth becomes a virtual prerequisite for most to join the board.

Affluence alone can bring someone to the attention of the board as a potential candidate, even in the absence of preexisting acquaintances. One wealthy woman, for instance, did not join the board through a friend or an acquaintance, but was approached "out of the blue." After coming to the attention of the institution because of her large contributions, she was approached by a board member who works closely with the development staff. She became increasingly involved with the organization and was eventually asked to join the board.

The elite character of the board is also perpetuated by current trustees' interest in maintaining board prestige, which both they and professional staff link to the organization's ability to raise money. In order to maintain prestige, they recruit people of stature in the eyes of other members of the elite. One trustee emphasized that, you need "important people to attract people" while another observed that certain members are included because "it looks good on our letterhead."

Yet another factor that promotes board homogeneity is a concern with recruiting members who "fit in" with the current board, and who can, as one nominating committee member put it, "get along with other people and be a team player." New trustees are expected to conform to current members' norms and values. One trustee feels that "wave makers" are not good for boards because they "cause a flap." Even a trustee who objects to some of the board members of newer wealth felt the board would not actually accept someone "offensive." Indeed, trustees repeatedly said they could not even remember a time that a controversial nomination had been made—although one could remember their having brought a "rough diamond" onto the board over twenty years ago. As one board leader explained, controversial names may come up (although none had during his experience) but "if they're that controversial, it's stopped in committee."

It is important to emphasize that trustees do think about the needs of their institutions as they see them when they recruit new members and take the process very seriously. Many men and women are invited to join the board only after they have participated in ways that show their commitment, capabilities, and familiarity with the institution, for example, on committees or advisory bodies. Boards also think about whether the candidate brings needed skills to the institution. The point, however, is that when they consider the needs of the organization and the board, they do so from within a class framework within which they recruit other members of the elite.

Shifts in Board Composition

To say that these boards perpetuate their character as *elite* boards does not mean that their composition remains the same. Shifting organizational circumstances and needs, as well as changes within the elite, help prompt shifts in recruitment criteria. These boards have become more diverse with respect to religious composition and expanded their inclusion of those with valued business skills. Today, all four boards say that they want to become more racially and ethnically diverse. The common theme, however, is that when these boards change, they typically do so by becoming more diverse *within* the elite, rather than by crossing class lines.

Elite boards are conservative, and shifts in board composition, like other types of change, are more readily accepted when trustees regard them as necessary for the health, and even the survival, of the organization. When trustees shift their recruitment criteria in response to organizational needs, however, they do it in ways that are shaped by their class. These points are illustrated by the shifting importance of religious boundaries on the boards.

The greater acceptance of Jews as trustees exemplifies how shifting circumstances prompt boards to become more inclusive *within* the elite. As I have shown elsewhere, prestigious boards became more open to Jewish donors, as well as formerly excluded "new" millionaires, in response to their organizations' need for funds. Jews and non-Jews on these boards acknowledge the importance of financial considerations in overcoming former barriers. As one put it, "in order to survive, they had to open up the doors." [19]

In both cities, the need for additional philanthropic funds contributed to bridging religious divisions, but at different stages of institutional development. In Orchid City, the boards of old and established institutions lowered existing barriers. Museum and opera trustees recalled the transition. One longtime (Protestant) trustee said,

> When I came on . . . [the board] was entirely the old-line WASP families, except for [one person] . . . But the composition of the board then evolved. We've attempted deliberately to do this . . . The old Protestant Establishment is still there, but very much only one of the players . . . The process has helped to shape that institution, and given it support it would not otherwise have gotten. And I can compare this experience with other institutions in this city, which have not taken that route, and have withered.

The board's evolution was facilitated by professional staff, who can also be important in current board efforts to increase racial and ethnic diversity.

Tulip City has also known barriers against Jews at elite institutions, such as social clubs. In that city, however, the barriers were crossed at the very founding of the museum and opera. A wealthy and prominent civic leader, who sought Jewish involvement in order to raise adequate philanthropic funds, played a critical role in the process. The importance of her role was recalled by both Jewish and non-Jewish trustees. One Jewish trustee said, "She was not having the kind of success she knew she should have, and she went to . . . someone in the Jewish community asking for their specific help. And once the doors were opened, we came out in droves." Indeed, the grandfather of another trustee was among those in the Jewish community that she approached for assistance. Other, non-Jewish donors also recalled how she welcomed in those who "had never been invited to the dance before." Another said that her approach was one reason adequate funds could be raised for the institutions. He said, "it was the first time that the Jews . . . [were] invited in . . . Anybody who wanted to come and be a donor was entitled to the same perks as the old guard." As the quote underscores, the "invitation" may have crossed religious boundaries, but it was directed toward those with the financial resources "to come and be a donor."

Today, all four boards say that they want to become more racially and ethnically diverse, a subject to be addressed in detail in chapter 3. At this point, however, we may note that the analysis of boards' approach to diversity reinforces the themes of this discussion. As we shall see, the level of attention and urgency that trustees attach to diversity efforts is heightened when they believe they are related to organizational survival. And as we shall also see, even as trustees seek greater racial and ethnic diversity, they also seek to remain within class boundaries.

Despite the differences in their communities' elites, age, and philanthropic traditions, the composition of the Orchid and Tulip City boards is similar because of a common emphasis on wealth as a criterion for membership. As DiMaggio and Useem (1982) point out, status-based exclusivity can come into conflict with organizational requirements for funds. Such tensions did indeed arise on the old and established Orchid City boards. Compared with Tulip City boards, the Orchid Museum and Opera (especially the former), still include a higher percentage of those with elite family backgrounds. Yet as these boards looked for new sources of money to support their costly institutions, trustees' financial concerns clearly worked to weaken status-based recruitment criteria (such as religion and family origins). The shift is reflected in the fact that the percentage of Orchid City board members listed in the *Social Register* dropped by over 40 percent in the course of two decades.[20] As this illustrates, boards select people on the basis of their elite status, but the relative emphasis given to various components of elite status are subject to change.

As long-time Orchid Opera trustees observed, the board used to be more cohesive and recruited from members of the same society bluebooks and clubs. Recalled one trustee, "they were a little clique." Trustees and professional staff alike observed that the board now includes more individuals who were chosen on the basis of personal wealth or corporate affiliation. A long-time trustee who said that the board used be drawn "from a narrower social level," explained, "Thirty years ago, you had people on the board who were not either major contributors or raising money—who were just there because they like opera and . . . knew somebody who got them on the board. It's harder to do that today."

One Jewish businessman, who was recruited to the board through business networks, described himself as one of the new types of people asked to join the board. He agrees that the board today is far less of a "blueblood" enclave, and attributed the board's shifting recruitment criteria to a "natural evolution that was tied to the expansion of the organization. The board became more professional, more businesslike."

As his comments suggest, organizational growth is an important consideration. So, too, is trustees' perception that it is now more difficult to find descendants of "old" families with the financial resources and interest to participate. Trustees, who connect organizational stature and size, have supported organizational growth that reflect their own aspirations, as well as those of professional staff. Their own goals, however, have contributed to the very conditions that require boards to adapt and incorporate new sources of funds and expertise.

As these institutions grow and seek additional funds, their operations have increasingly come to resemble those of a business. An evolution in the board's view of the institution as a business is chronicled in annual reports, as well as in trustee comments. One annual report, for instance, explains that a change in financial accounting procedures was necessary because the organization's operations now resemble those of a complex business. These changes also enhance the value that boards place on business skills in recruiting new members. For instance, a nominating committee member explained that when the institution expanded its retailing operations to generate revenue, they also recruited a top executive with retailing expertise to the board. We shall return to examine further shifts in recruitment and composition related to changes in organizational circumstances and board roles in chapters 3 and 4.

Equally important is that boards can also become *more* exclusive with respect to their elite recruitment criteria. While all of these boards emphasize financial resources, they stop short of "selling" board seats, at least explicitly, for to do so would undermine the very prestige that makes them so desirable. The extent to which boards can be selective, of course, depends on the number of individuals interested in membership. In that respect, these boards want to be desirable to as many affluent people as possible. Members of the newest organization, the Tulip Opera, for instance, approvingly noted the increasing desirability of their board. Said one member of the nominating committee, "It's a matter of making choices now, because certainly there are enough candidates who would like to serve . . . And that might not have been the case 10 years ago." Thus, even as a need for money prompts greater openness at the older Orchid City institutions, the enhanced prestige of this newer Tulip City board allowed it to, like its counterparts, "make choices now."

As we can see, these institutions do indeed have elite boards, that preserve their exclusivity. They do so even as the boards have become open in other ways, and this duality is the subject to which we now turn.

CHAPTER TWO

A Dual Approach:
Openness and Exclusivity on the Elite Board

Class influences the selection of candidates that boards recruit as members and the value that those elite members place on joining the board. Once on the board as trustees, however, elites are faced with the organizational needs and pressures of the institutions they govern. While the influences of class and organization are sometimes complementary, they often stand in tension. Although class-based influences promote exclusivity and traditionalism, organizational circumstances may require greater openness and receptivity to change. In response, trustees adapt, but in a way that is influenced by class.

Trustees accommodate the dual influences of class and organization by developing a bifurcation in their own outlook, functioning on two related but distinct tracks. In order to address organizational needs, trustees take certain stances concerning organizational operations and accessibility that are surprisingly at odds with traditional images of elite exclusivity. At the same time, they retain a separate and exclusive niche for their own involvement with the institution, including the board. Others may use the institution, and indeed, trustees support measures designed to expand audiences. Elites, however, involve themselves in a distinctive way that permits them to retain a special sense of identification with the institution.

Moreover, while they make accommodations, they do so in ways that preserve their understanding of the organization's mission and stature.

The way that trustees think and act, including the duality in their approach, is shaped by how they view involvement with the arts and arts institutions. Trustees value the arts, but involvement with these arts institutions also has a status-related significance that is above and beyond their aesthetic activities. Both aesthetic and status-related values heighten the desirability of associating with these institutions and their boards. Trustees seek to preserve the stature of both the board and the institution, which they expect to represent "the best" within its field. As they do so, trustees contribute to the very organizational growth and heightened financial needs that require them to adapt.

Trustees' Esteem for the Arts

Trustees' outlook and activities reflect both aesthetic and status-related concerns and meanings that they bring to the board. An interest in art and the prestige of arts board membership are relevant to why affluent individuals join boards and to how they function as trustees, including their patterns of openness and exclusivity.

Trustees expressed their enjoyment of art and their belief in the importance of the organization's artistic mission. Thus, one museum trustee serves on the board because, "I'm very interested in art," and another said "I'm in love with the institution." Opera trustees often spoke in expansive terms, using words like "love" and "passion" to describe their feelings about opera. Opera boards often conveyed the feeling of enthusiastic (albeit elite) fan clubs. Indeed, one opera trustee described himself as "a groupie when it comes to opera singers." Trustees pursue their artistic interests in ways that reflect (and often require) their affluence. Indeed, membership on elite arts boards, which carries expectations of large donations, is itself a case in point. Additional examples include collecting art and traveling to attend opera performances nationally and internationally.

Although an appreciation of art was widespread, levels of interest and involvement varied among trustees. Many people contrasted themselves with those for whom art was a more consuming focus. For instance, one opera trustee said, "I don't consider myself a real aficionado. I mean, historically, I was the kind of person who went to the opera 8 times in a season . . . I got to a point where I had a subscription, but not where I passionately follow the thing . . . I'm not one of those. There are people on the board who are—but not many."

Trustees enjoy art but do not necessarily claim considerable artistic knowledge or background, nor do they expect it of fellow board members. One opera trustee said, "I do not represent myself as an expert on the opera anymore than I'm an expert on cancer . . . Nor do I want to be thought of as an expert." A museum trustee emphasized, "I don't know much about art. I'm no art historian. And my taste is only as refined as I know what I like when I see it." In the view of one European trustee, "the overall degree of knowledge of the [American] board is lower than it would be in [his native country]." Trustees do, however, admire those with artistic expertise, and, for some, the opportunity to learn more about art was one of the rewards of board service.

What trustees do express and expect, however, is a concern for the institution and its mission. One trustee said, "Many of the trustees don't know anything about art, but they know the institution should exist." When a new chair was selected for another board, the various criteria used by the selection committee did not include expertise in art but did require, in the words of one committee member, "an ongoing interest and affection for the place." A man who is "not famous for either my art collection or my knowledge of abstract expressionism" said he serves on the board because he is "interested in maintaining this incredible storehouse and educational institution of the arts." As for the man who is "no art historian," he praised his institution's mission as one of "nourishing souls," while the opera trustee who is not an "aficionado" believes that her institution "makes a difference to the world."

Trustees, Arts Institutions, and Prestige

Elites are drawn to these institutions not only out of an interest and belief in their artistic mission, but because of the prestige associated with their boards among members of their class. Board status and organizational status are intertwined. Boards derive prestige from their elite members, association with the arts, and the stature of the institutions in their fields. One museum trustee said his board is prestigious because it attracts "big names that people like to feel they're somewhere in the area of." Another trustee derives a certain "psychic" satisfaction from board membership, because "it's a prestige institution, and it's nice to be on the board of the number one institution in the city." Opera trustees similarly commented on board prestige. One characterized membership on her board as "a real plum," and many noted the "elegance" and "cachet" associated with opera, such as a man who observed that people are attracted to the opera board "for a lot of different reasons. Some people like opera. Some people like parties. Some people like glitz." A Tulip

City trustee who feels that "art and culture give a certain status," believes that art is "very special" and that "being part of a museum *should* be viewed as a prestigious appointment."

Trustees and professionals characterize prestige as an important tool for attracting people to the board who are able and willing to make large donations. Said one, "the prestige attracts money." Indeed, people approach these boards with offers of large donations in exchange for board membership. Although these boards use wealth as a criterion for recruitment, they also stop short of explicitly selling seats, which would dilute the very stature that makes them so desirable. An opera trustee believes her board is "at the top of the list" in terms of prestige, because "you can't buy your way onto it." She acknowledged, "money has everything to do with [the organization]," but added that you cannot make a deal to join: "I know that from people who wanted to make a deal, and it just doesn't work like that. You have to demonstrate . . . that your heart is in the right place." Said the head of another board, "we have a rule on the nominating committee that we can't be bought." Prestigious boards can simultaneously make wealth a criteria for membership and still use other considerations because so many wealthy people want to join.

The outlook among the trustees of these four boards concerning art and arts institutions reflects a more widespread value and prestige associated with the arts in elite philanthropy. Affluent patrons have been influential in founding and supporting arts organizations in numerous American cities. The upper-class composition of arts boards in varied cities and regions further testifies to elite involvement in cultural institutions.[1] In a study of elite philanthropy, for instance, I found that culture was a major recipient of philanthropy among New York donors.

These donors perceived a prestige hierarchy among nonprofit boards and institutions, and arts institutions were among those at the top.[2] The prominence of culture is a distinctive feature of *elite* philanthropy, for culture is a relatively minor recipient of charitable giving in general.[3]

Exclusivity and the Arts

Historical research indicates that elites have not only valued the arts, but that they have sought to monopolize art and arts institutions that they supported within their group.[4] Elite arts boards have resisted the extension of organizational services even to the upper-middle class. DiMaggio documents monopolization efforts by Boston's upper-class arts patrons, and elite influence also moved art and arts institutions toward greater exclusivity in other cities.[5] Indeed, DiMaggio and Useem observe that elite boards "often greeted with a certain dismay evidence of rising popular interest in the arts." As late as the 1960s, for instance, one symphony board refused to endorse a public concert series. Similarly, an opera board disapproved of the professional director's efforts to dispel opera's elitist image.[6] Smith characterizes another opera as historically resembling a "closed corporation": It was almost impossible to learn about performances, the institution rarely advertised, and occasional small ads that did appear generally included the words "sold out."[7]

The attitudes of contemporary trustees in this study contrast with such historical patterns of exclusivity. As trustees themselves are aware, times have changed, and the institutions that they value can no longer be sustained by any small group of wealthy patrons. To preserve these large and costly organizations at the level they desire, elites must attract wider support, and their attitudes reflect that recognition. So, too, do the annual reports of the institutions, in which growing financial needs and board efforts to devise new strategies to meet them are an ongoing theme. Faced with heightened organizational needs for funds, elites adapt—accepting, and even encouraging measures designed to expand audiences and exhibiting a greater openness in relation to organizational services and operations.

Elites and Audience Expansion: The Case of "Supertitles"

The introduction of supertitles, which provide English translations during opera performances, provides a striking instance of trustee support for a measure intended to attract a wider audience. The very purpose of supertitles is to make opera more accessible and trustees support their use precisely because they are seen as a way to "get more people interested." Attracting more people, in turn, is seen as critical to maintaining the economic viability of the opera. One trustee went so far as to hail supertitles as "the greatest contribution to opera." Said another, "I really think that's helped a lot of new opera goers. They really enjoy it, because they know what's going on." Even a trustee who previously was opposed to using titles said that she wound up "eating my words, because . . . the public want them." Similarly, a trustee who personally finds supertitles "distracting" said she supports their use because they attract more people, by making performances no longer feel like listening to a language you cannot understand. Trustees also say that because they make opera more accessible, supertitles contribute to the long-term health of opera by making people more willing to attend lesser-known operas. As one trustee explained, this permits the opera to expand its repertory, which is important because an overdependence on the "hits" (such as *La Bohème*) ultimately leads to a decline in artistic quality.

Trustees' endorsement of supertitles exemplifies their belief that the continued viability of the organizations and art form they value is dependent on attracting a wider audience, and they make accommodations accordingly. Indeed, it was after receiving a large volume of requests for supertitles that one board was prompted to focus on the issue. As this illustrates, trustees felt they had to be responsive to a wider public. At the Orchid Opera, which is wealthier and more established than the Tulip, trustees adopted supertitles with greater caution, and greater concern that supertitles be done "tastefully." Still, although done more slowly and with greater selectivity, supertitles were adopted because patrons wanted them.

Marketing and Retail Activities

Commercial forces tend to erode exclusive status boundaries and distribute culture more widely and have often been viewed as debasing art.[8] Historically elites have sought to insulate high cultural institutions and art from the "contaminating" influence of market forces. Although marketing and retail activities (such as museum shops) conflict with earlier and more clublike ways of operating, they respond to the increased need for funds faced today by large cultural organizations. Albeit ambivalently at times, the trustees of these four boards accept commercial activities as an accommodation to that reality, as a way to generate additional funds. The case of the Orchid Museum, which developed an extensive series of merchandising and marketing activities to generate income, exemplifies how and why trustees make such an accommodation. One long-time trustee reflected the evolution on his board in this area and the economic circumstances they faced. He recalled that when he first joined the board, a family member (and previous trustee) told him,

"This . . . institution . . . is so well endowed, you'll never have to raise money." But, he said, "I know, [millions of dollars] later . . . that proved not to be right."

Even within a few years of his joining the board, the gap between expenses and income was mounting sharply. Today, the percent of operating expenses that this museum can fund through endowment interest is less than half of what it was when he became a trustee. One way that the board tried to generate additional funds was by initiating a series of retailing activities. The trustee recalled, "You heard voices when we started this, 'You're just going to become another department store.' And I suppose some people would still say that a first rate cultural institution shouldn't have to do this kind of thing. But you have to survive." Another board member said she initially did think that these activities were "too commercialized," but changed her mind after seeing how much money they earned for the museum. Now, she says, "institutions must adapt." Yet another emphasized the necessity of these ventures for "the bottom line." Those making such comments include descendants of upper-class families, who might be expected to oppose commercial activities most strongly.

To say that trustees now endorse commercial activities does not mean that they have lost all connotations of crassness, and trustees insist they be done "tastefully." The boundaries they draw between what is and is not "tasteful" have weakened, however, and an accommodation has been made that allows trustees to support, and participate in, such activities. The level of board acceptance is further illustrated by the fact that the museum board now has a distinct committee to deal with commercial ventures, and recruited new members who possessed retailing expertise.

The boundaries between art and commercialism are further weakened as trustees characterize these arts organizations as businesses, which have to be marketed like any other business. A member of the Tulip Opera board's marketing committee explained that their purpose is "to sell the opera." A Tulip Art Museum trustee observed that the institution had not been "marketed properly" in the past, a fact now viewed as a flaw in need of correction. Trustees with advertising and marketing experience saw their background as the basis of a contribution they could make as board members, such as one who took on an audience development project for the organization and approached it as a "marketing problem." As for the opera that rarely advertised described by Smith (see above), by the 1980s, "what was once a closed corporation now trumpeted ticket availability in newspapers, on radio, and through the mails."[9]

Board Exclusivity: The Other Side of the Duality

While trustees' attitudes are surprisingly open with respect to organizational services and operations, when it comes to the board itself, other attitudes perpetuate exclusivity. It is not that trustees seek to monopolize the organization's artistic services, but they do preserve a separate and exclusive niche for their own involvement, which brings them together with one another and the organization in ways shaped by their class. It is the way that elites involve themselves with these organizations that is exclusive and that perpetuates the class-related prestige associated with the organizations.

Central to the elite enclave surrounding these institutions is the board itself, which remains exclusive in composition. Emphasizing just how homogeneous a board can be, one trustee was led to remark, "the trustees are clones of each other." The way that board recruitment is conducted, and the emphasis that trustees place on raising and contributing money as a trustee role, makes affluence a virtual necessity for membership. These also contribute to the culture of wealth that suffuses these boards.

Boards consciously take measures to maintain their prestige. They recruit prominent people who attract other wealthy people who want to interact with them and feel that they are members of the same group. As one trustee said, socially prominent trustees such as Mary Doe, a member of his board, make other wealthy people want to join so that they can say, "Well, Mary and I were discussing this the other day, or whatever." By the end of the interview (and perhaps illustrating his own point), this man had recounted his own involvement with this prestigious trustee.

Boards also seek to maintain prestige by holding social and fundraising events in elegant and exclusive settings, in which trustees interact with one another and other affluent donors. These settings include the homes of wealthy trustees, and the organization itself (when closed to the general public). Even when the institution is open to the public, special rooms exist to which only trustees and major donors have access. Entree to exclusive social events and venues is itself a reward of trusteeship. For instance, one museum trustee said he shouldn't make board membership "sound entirely eleemosynary, because you do get some nice perks, such as invitations to openings and so on." An opera trustee said he particularly enjoyed attending small parties he is invited to attend because he is on the board. Among the guests at one such party, held in the home of a very wealthy individual, were opera singers who performed in this intimate setting. "How many people," he asked, "have the opportunity to do something as interesting as that?"

Creating occasions for trustees to interact with artists and experience art in exclusive settings is another mechanism used by boards to maintain prestige. Thus, asked whether his board does anything to maintain its prestige, one opera trustee said, "Oh, sure. They're good at having receptions with artists. I'm going to one tonight . . . [It] makes everyone feel part of it." A museum trustee characterized the opportunity to see art "without the crowds" as one of the "privileges" of board membership.

The exclusive way that elites interact with each other and the institution cultivates a heightened and special sense of identification with the organizations, even though others may also use the institution. One trustee explained that serving on the board provides, "the opportunity to just see close up so many things I might not have otherwise seen, and to be a part of them. To feel that you are really part of something very important, very interesting, very wonderful." Boards consciously try to cultivate a sense of belonging among affluent donors and trustees because it encourages them to support the organization financially. Indeed, many trustees candidly said they would not contribute, or would contribute at lower levels, if they were not members of the board.

Conclusion: Organizational Needs, Money, and Class Exclusivity

Faced with heightened organizational need for funds, affluent trustees exhibit a receptivity to organizational accessibility and change that is surprisingly at odds with traditional images of elite exclusivity. The fact that elites are willing to adapt testifies both to the concern they have for the health of the organizations, as well as to their view of how the institutions should survive. These trustees do not merely want their institutions to stay in existence, but to function at the top of their fields, a goal that requires infusions of money beyond what a small group of affluent donors can or will provide.

Trustees' vision of the organization contributes to the very organizational demands that require them to adapt, but it also sets limits on how far they will go. This is illustrated by the comments of a leading trustee at one of the operas. Although the opera now engages in formerly unthinkable levels and forms of retailing activities, he emphasized that one survival strategy they will *not* pursue is to convert the institution itself to "mass entertainment"—by which he meant such things as performing operettas. Trustees are willing to adapt to ensure the survival and stature of the organization, but the way in which the institution survives must conform to their vision of its mission and stature.

Elite boards define their goal conservatively, as one of preserving the institution and its mission in perpetuity. It is when they believe that organizational survival and stature are at stake that they are most receptive to change. Yet even as elites make accommodations to the reality of large-scale organization, they do so in a way that preserves the status-related values associated with their own involvement in the arts. Elites carve out a separate niche for themselves in relation to these organizations, and when it comes to the board itself, exclusivity prevails.

At times, the organizational need for funds does come into conflict with board exclusivity. This occurs, for instance, when "old guard" trustees resist admitting millionaires (such as Jewish donors in the past) with the financial resources to contribute, but who are seen as outside of their social group. Trustees can and have addressed this tension, though, by becoming more open *within* the elite. Indeed, the commercial activities trustees support in order to generate more funds also have consequences for board composition, as in the Orchid Museum's introduction of businesspeople with retailing expertise not previously found on the board. Once again, it is a shift that widens the boundaries of inclusion within the elite. In such cases, it is a broadening in emphasis and/or shift in the types of elite resources sought (e.g., social and family prominence versus economic resources or business expertise), but continuity in that the resources sought are still those possessed by elites.

More business-oriented trustees who have varying degrees of closeness to traditional upper-class families may be more likely to focus on the institution's business needs, but they share common values about the organization with more socially oriented members and see a role for status-oriented concerns. One CEO, for instance, said his institution has "any number of functions, and people love to go and sashay around." Although these events are not his "bag," he believes that they are important because they attract money to the institution.

Ironically, when trustees legitimate the exclusivity of the board with respect to wealth, they make reference to the very organizational needs that prompt them to become more open with respect to organizational accessibility. Trustees emphasize that giving and raising money must be a central board function because of the enormous economic needs of these costly institutions. Accordingly, they view wealth as an important factor in recruiting board members. Expressing a commonly held view, one trustee said, "I think it always helps to have rich people on a board . . . You know, you need money to run these institutions . . . And the more rich people you have involved, the more chance you have of raising money from them." This trustee is himself very wealthy and clearly was not troubled by the board's exclusivity with respect to class. But even one unusual trustee who was less affluent and very uncomfortable with the class character of her board said, "The problem of the [organization] is that it is immense, and so they must raise a lot of money, and therefore need to have rich people on the board." Whatever the motive, and whether it is conscious or not, trustees' emphasis on fundraising and recruiting the affluent has the consequence of perpetuating the exclusivity of the board.

One long-time museum director observes that in the past, some wealthy patrons approached the museum as "a kind of aesthetic country club." [10] Some trustees feel that this attitude can still be found among certain individuals, but the more typical view is that these museums and operas are today analogous to large and complex businesses. Many trustees also clearly want to feel that they support an institution that provides a public service in their minds, and not an exclusive club. Still, the way in which they choose to do so is from within an exclusive enclave. Boards are not "country clubs" but they are indeed prestigious, selective, and elite, and both their elite character and the needs of these businesslike institutions shape how elite boards govern.

Diversity and the Elite Board:
Race, Ethnicity, and Class

We are looking for diversity. You can't be an all white board, and you can't be an all white institution any longer . . . We're a very visible institution in a big town that's changing . . . and I just don't want to see us get into trouble . . . It's the right thing to do, and also, we're missing a good chance at getting some very good people.

A major insight of elite theory is that elites and their institutions must change if they are to survive.[1] As the preceding comments of a white trustee indicate, today these boards are addressing their (and their institutions') ability to adapt by becoming more racially and ethnically diverse. Members of all four boards, characterize diversity as something they support, believe is important, and regard as an increasingly necessary focus of attention. Trustees of varied ethnic backgrounds say that there are indeed cases in which these boards have welcomed members of minorities into their ranks. Nonetheless, all four boards remain overwhelmingly white,[2] a homogeneity made all the more stark by the ethnic and racial diversity of their surrounding cities. These boards may not be "all white," but they come close.

This chapter examines trustees' approach to their stated goal of diversity in relation to the dual influences of class and organization. Attention to diversity has been spurred by concerns about the organization's financial needs, public image, and relations with the wider community. This is reflected in the fact that in Tulip City, where diversity has more closely and explicitly been linked to organizational needs than in Orchid City, it was also the subject of more widespread and pronounced attention. Trustees from both cities say that they believe that responding to a changing social environment is also the "responsible" and the "right" thing to do.

Elite boards are not the only boards that are racially and ethnically homogeneous or that are broaching the subject of greater diversity.[3] Their character as *elite* boards, however, is reflected in how they approach the issue. Attention to organizational concerns in the light of societal changes put diversity on the boards' agenda, but class-related influences shape their response. Efforts at greater ethnic inclusivity are coupled with continued class exclusivity. Whatever the ethnic or racial identity of the individuals they seek to recruit, these boards typically look to those who are affluent and who have connections to those with economic, social, and political resources. Indeed, all of these boards would far more readily recruit an affluent businessperson of African, Asian, or Hispanic descent than a poor or working-class white person of European origins.

An ongoing theme of this book is the bifurcation that characterizes trustees' outlook, in which greater openness with respect to the organization is coupled with class exclusivity with respect to the board. That bifurcation is also reflected in how these boards approach diversity. On the one hand, trustees accept, and indeed support, organizational programs and services addressed to members of minority groups of varied economic backgrounds. Yet when it comes to the board itself, class exclusivity prevails, as they focus on recruiting those who are elite.

As this suggests, elite boards' efforts at diversity may represent change, but it is change that is undertaken within a larger continuity. Board attention to diversity is reactive in the sense that, however willingly done, it represents a response to wider societal changes and forces. To a considerable degree, however, the way that boards respond is on their own terms, by extending their existing recruitment priorities and criteria to a new group. This is not only a question of recruiting those who are affluent, but who are perceived to "fit" in the prevailing board culture and practices. Whatever the racial or ethnic background of those being recruited, whether white or not, trustees seek to avoid those who they fear will "cause a flap."

An important implication of this continuity in how boards approach diversity is that we cannot assume that changes in board composition translate into other types of changes or diversity. Indeed, many white trustees' receptivity to greater diversity would likely weaken were it to become associated with substantial changes in the character of the board and organization. It is nonetheless true that, particularly in Tulip City, trustees have linked diversity efforts to adaptations in the nature of the services provided by the organization. The question, however, is just how far trustees would be willing to see either the board or the organization change, were that to be perceived as a correlate of greater diversity.

This chapter also considers the significance of ethnic identity in relation to board service from the point of view of those African-Americans and Hispanics (the two minority groups included) who are members of these boards. The homogeneity of these boards raises the question of whether those minorities who do serve experience acceptance or barriers related to their ethnic identity, once on the board. A further major question is whether or not these trustees link their racial or ethnic identity to what they actually do as trustees. After all, trustees have many interests and potential sources of identity from which to draw, that include ethnicity, but also class, occupation, and an interest in supporting civic institutions. As we shall see, there is no uniform answer, but the answers that do emerge speak to the relationship between demographic and operational change on the boards.

Organizational Needs, Context, and Attention to Diversity

Trustees typically believe that the evolution of their cities and the country as a whole has made diversity an issue of prominence that needs to be addressed. The growing ethnic and racial diversity of the city's population and political leaders, experience with diversity-related issues in the workplace, public and private grantmakers' interest in board diversity, and assessments of general societal expectations all contribute to focusing trustee attention in this direction. As one Orchid City trustee said, his nominating committee discusses how to diversify because "you can't live in a vacuum." Said a Tulip City board member, "There's a sense of responsibility, and there's an imposed responsibility . . . that everybody who's sort of involved in how this society works is stressing." Although many trustees say they welcome greater diversity, external social changes have been instrumental in prompting its arrival on the agenda. As the opening quote suggests, there is the sense that in today's society, failure to respond could "get us into trouble."

Diversity has become an issue that trustees of all four boards believe must be addressed, but there is a striking difference in the frequency and manner with which it is discussed in the two cities. Tulip City board members were more likely to raise the subject on their own, to discuss it at greater length, and to view it with a heightened sense of urgency. They were also more likely to discuss diversity as something that could benefit the organization. Tulip City trustees were also far more likely to express interest, knowledge, and enthusiasm concerning the organization's outreach programs. In Tulip City, but not in Orchid City, diversity was among the most prominent themes in the interviews. Why should this be the case?

In Tulip City, demographic changes have led trustees to conclude that greater ethnic and racial inclusivity has actually become a matter of organizational survival. Furthermore, Tulip City institutions do not have as wide or established a base of support as do Orchid City institutions, and thus feel a more acute need to expand that base. In Tulip City, as in Orchid City, trustees clearly believe that greater diversity is both a societal expectation and the "right" thing to do, with consequences for organizational legitimacy in the city. But in Tulip City trustees also express the sense that diversity is instrumental in achieving internally set goals and to obtaining the financial resources critical to the organization's future. Repeatedly, Tulip City trustees said that the demographics of the city had changed so dramatically that they must attract the participation and financial support of individuals of diverse ethnic groups to maintain these costly institutions. Thus, one museum trustee said,

> [Tulip City] is dramatically changing—the influences here, the cultures here . . . We're here to serve the community, so we had better take off any blinders, and open

43

up the opportunities . . . You just have to do it to survive. It affects your fundraising. It affects your image in the community . . . The board has to think that way too . . . We need more minority representation on the board.

Another museum trustee explained that as the community changed, the board's thinking evolved to a "recognition that money comes in all colors and sizes."

Similar comments were made by trustees of the Tulip Opera. One trustee, said, "You can't live [here] without seeing the change in the ethnic diversity of the, of the whole community." In light of this change, she said, "we are realizing that we have to, we have to, become more multicultural if we're going to survive." Accordingly, the inclusion of trustees from other ethnic and racial groups, "is dealing with the reality of life here."

A Tulip Opera initiative illustrates well how efforts at diversity are sparked by the perceived consequences of wider societal changes for the organization. Attracting additional support from varied ethnic and racial communities is all the more important for the opera because of plans to expand their program, necessitating that they enlarge their audience and financial resources. Tulip City's large Hispanic population is seen as one important such community. One trustee succinctly concludes that, "if the Opera's going to continue, Hispanics have got to like opera." Thus, professional staff, seeking to widen their support base, approached a Hispanic volunteer, and asked her to lead an effort to involve other affluent Hispanics with the opera.[4] She agreed, was successful, and trustees invited her to join the board.

The Tulip Opera example represents an unusual case of

board progress toward diversity. It also suggests that just as external prompting brought diversity onto the agenda, external assistance may well be necessary to implement that agenda, for professional staff were critical in enlisting the volunteer's help. Similarly, the initiative itself rested on the input and guidance of someone who was not on the board, and whose own ethnic background, unlike the majority of white trustees, gave her a link to one of the very communities they hoped to reach.

Trustees themselves often say that it is very hard to find minority members to give and/or raise money. Yet these boards have also proved unsuccessful in initiating and undertaking the actions needed to find and recruit those who *are* available. This reflects the insularity of the networks and perspectives found within the board, a subject to which we will return. Proactive efforts by professional staff can be key under these circumstances. At the Tulip Opera, the board welcomed such efforts.

Class Exclusivity and Ethnic and Racial Diversity

If environmental and organizational considerations direct trustees' attention to diversity-related issues, class-based influences shape their response. Even as they seek greater inclusivity with respect to race and ethnicity, when it comes to the board, they remain exclusive with respect to class. As we have seen in chapter 1, virtually all the Hispanic and black trustees were millionaires or multimillionaires. Interestingly, a Hispanic trustee, and one of the few non-millionaires of any ethnicity, is no longer on his board. That same board has recruited another Hispanic member, however—one who is quite wealthy.

These arts boards do recruit some men and women of color who are not in a position to be large donors, as is also true of some white trustees. Their goal in selecting trustees of any race or ethnicity, however, is to recruit those of considerable means.[5] This directly reflects how these elite trustees define the board, its functions, and its responsibilities. It also reflects their emphasis on bringing in the resources that will allow them not only to sustain these institutions, but to sustain them as *elite* institutions within their fields. When trustees seek to diversify, they simply extend their same criteria and priorities to new groups. As one white trustee said, his board would "love" to have more ethnic and racial diversity, as long as those recruited are "wealthy and respected and think the way we do."

The emphasis on recruiting those of affluence is not only a matter of obtaining those with economic resources, but of including those who current trustees think will "fit" within the board's existing culture and mode of operation, which is deeply shaped by class. This is reflected in the comments of an African-American trustee, who described his board's resistance to crossing class lines as follows:

> [This] is still a pretty stuffy board . . . The people who have their hands on the controls are by and large socialites. They're wealthy, patrons of the arts, lead a certain life . . . So going out and dragging in a couple guys from [a poor minority neighborhood] just wouldn't work . . . While boards like [this] have convinced themselves that "Yes we're looking, diversity is important" . . . Still, they want somebody who talks and acts and dresses more like they do, than like many of the people who they purport to want to bring in . . . And in fact they are also looking for people who can make a contribution. Not just a monetary contribution, but who bring something to the party.

Yet he does believe that his and similar boards will become more diverse, but that this will occur "as more and more blacks and other minorities . . . permeate all of the class levels of society," thus enlarging their presence among the economic elite.

The comments of another, white, trustee, illustrate just how natural it is for these trustees to think along class lines. A member of the professional staff was concerned about the fact there was a room in the organization whose use was reserved for large donors. But, the trustee said, "It didn't worry me—because it was so democratic that it didn't matter what your background was, it didn't matter where your money came from, if you gave, you were welcome . . . And we were happy to see you."

As this quote indicates, even when trustees speak about being inclusive, they generally mean with respect to those who have the money to contribute. Although they would say it is wrong to exclude people from the board based on their race, ethnicity, or gender, the legitimacy of class exclusivity is basically a nonissue. A rare trustee who does want to see more class diversity sees no support for his view among other trustees.

Whatever questions one might raise about the depth and effectiveness of their diversity efforts, any of these boards would more readily recruit a wealthy person of color than a poor or working-class white person. Racial and ethnic heterogeneity represent an adaptation, but one that trustees can accommodate within their larger framework, priorities, and way of operating. By contrast, class heterogeneity would necessitate that trustees redefine their role and that would be in tension with the entire culture within which the board functions. In sum, class diversity would constitute a more radical change, that would go outside the very nature of the philanthropic system within which these boards and the organizations function.

Minority Trustees on the Board:
Acceptance or Marginalization?

To this point, the discussion has focused on the recruitment of trustees from more varied ethnic and racial groups to these boards. In so doing, we have given attention to the perspective of those who currently predominate, namely, white trustees. In this and the following section, we explore whether and how Hispanic and African-American trustees characterize their ethnic identity as significant for their participation. This section begins by examining whether or not these men and women feel they are integrated members of the board or whether they experience isolation or barriers to participation that they see as rooted in racial and ethnic differences from the white majority.

Virtually every minority trustee said they felt accepted and able to actively participate.[6] For instance, a Hispanic trustee said, "I have had all the access to the power positions within the board . . . I'm on several key committees where my voice can be heard, and normally I get a good reaction to my initiatives." Similar sentiments were expressed by a black member of another board, who felt the board would welcome his additional involvement, which he had to resist at present because of heavy business obligations. Significantly, he attributed the ease of his interaction with white trustees to their shared class position. He said:

> I don't have any problem with any of the people, because at the end of the day it's very easy to forget that I'm a black person because I don't wear my hat backwards or carry a loud radio. And they say, after a fashion, "Oh, he's just like us," and everything proceeds after that as if he were just like us. And that's a manifestation of class.

Even an African-American trustee who criticized his board as making inadequate efforts toward greater diversity and expressed considerable frustration with fellow trustees on this subject, also felt that he personally was very much accepted and integrated within the board. He has served on, and chaired, major committees, and said "I have quite a bit of influence . . . They respect what I do, and they consult with me. I participate in the smaller . . . discussions that go on over lunch." With some dismay, he said, "I am one of them."

Some black and Hispanic trustees did say that they could not be more active, but ascribed this to choices that they had made because of factors unconnected to race or ethnicity. For instance, black and Hispanic businesspeople said that business activities precluded further involvement—a sentiment also expressed by many white businesspeople.

Racial and Ethnic Identity and the Trustee Role: Views of African-American and Hispanic Board Members

Do black and Hispanic members of the board connect their ethnic identity to their outlook and activities as trustees? After all, trustees have other potential sources of identity (such as class and occupation), and interests (in art, supporting civic institutions) which may shape how they conceive of their niche and contributions on the board. Even among this small group of individuals and boards, the answer that emerges is that there is no single answer. Rather, it varies among individuals, including those within the same ethnic group (i.e., Hispanics and African-Americans) and within the same boards. While the numbers are far too small to permit systematic analyses or conclusions about what may account for these variations, the material suggests two possibilities that bear further investigation, the trustee's occupation and city.

To convey the variation that exists, it is useful to compare the comments of trustees who did with the comments of those who did not link their ethnic identity to their outlook and role as trustees. Among the former is a Hispanic trustee, who said, "What I do . . . is to express a point of view which has been formed through a different environment." He emphasized that he is not "a monothematic spokesperson" and does not "represent anyone but myself, but . . . I think I do understand what would make Latinos go" to this institution. At the same time, he noted, "there's a lot of commonality," between his point of view and that of fellow trustees, such as their mutual interest in art.

An African-American trustee linked trustees' ethnic identity to their ability to carry out certain board roles. He believes that the board's responsibilities include "leading by example in terms of diversity," which "sets the tone" for professional staff and outreach programs. Today, he said, his board "needs to get out" but doing so requires more diversity within their own ranks. Affluent white trustees, he said, "have no idea of what is going on [in minority communities], so how can they do outreach?" He too, sees race and ethnicity as one influence, but not the exclusive one, and indeed made it clear that he would be offended at the idea that his racial identity alone was determinative of how he approached his role.

In contrast to these examples are another two trustees, also one Hispanic and one African-American. While the previous two were both in professional occupations outside of business, both of these men were in business. Unlike the previous two, these trustees did not refer to race or ethnicity when talking about their own role as trustees, or to the boards' role more generally. They did, however, link their board roles to their business and financial background. Thus, the Hispanic trustee spoke of the financial resources he is able to donate to the institution and of the relevance of his business skills to performing certain board functions. Similarly, the black trustee, who serves on finance-related committees, characterized his niche within the board as influenced by his business expertise. Such comments were quite similar to those made by many white businesspeople.

These two businessmen do not distance themselves from, or express indifference to, racial or ethnic affiliations. To the contrary, both have other philanthropic involvements in their ethnic communities. The point is rather that they draw on other aspects of their lives in thinking about what they do and contribute on these particular boards. The economic and business resources that they draw on are precisely those that are so highly valued within these boards.

In contrast to these two trustees, the first two were in professions outside of business, and their technical skills are not similarly related to board tasks, at least as currently defined. Other examples also fit this pattern of variation. There was, however, also one former businessperson who drew on both ethnic identity and business skills in discussing her trustee role. Whether the link between trustees' occupation and the likelihood of their connecting ethnic identity to their board role would hold up under additional scrutiny remains to be seen, but it is an issue warranting further investigation.

Also noteworthy was that all of the Tulip City trustees connected ethnic identity to their role as trustees. Still, so too did one of the Orchid City trustees (who was also not a businessperson). In Orchid City, a Hispanic trustee, who in fact placed more importance on ethnic identity than did any other black or

Hispanic trustee, did not feel this fit well into a trustee role. By contrast, Hispanic trustees in Tulip City felt that their ethnic identity put them in a position to carry out their roles in ways that represented the goals and priorities of the board as a whole. Again, though it is premature to say, it may well be that the centrality of diversity issues within Tulip City heightens the chances that individual minority members will draw on their ethnic identity in approaching their trustee role, for these boards have more explicitly defined developing relationships with members of additional ethnic and racial communities as a role that they value. Indeed, one trustee specifically went onto the board because of board interest in his ideas about diversity and outreach. The Hispanic woman who led the Tulip Opera's initiative did not become involved with the opera because of her ethnic identity. Yet the organization's interest in attracting the Hispanic community eventually resulted in her emergence as a trustee focused on making such connections, a role she very much values.

In reality, the relationship (or absence of a relation) between trustees' ethnic identity and what they think and do as trustees on these boards is likely to involve numerous and interacting influences. It is important to note, however, that the paucity of cases that prevents us from more thoroughly scrutinizing these, is not merely a methodological or sampling problem that remains to be overcome. Rather, it reflects the actual scarcity of minorities on these boards. Indeed, it is quite possible that were greater diversity to occur, and those numbers to substantially increase, the very relationship between ethnic identity and how trustees see their role might change as well.

Barriers to Diversification

Class exclusivity shapes how these boards approach diversity, but it also contributes to their racial and ethnic homogeneity. These boards draw their members from an economic elite of top corporate executives and the very wealthy. Whites of non-Hispanic descent predominate in those positions,[7] as they do on these arts boards. As this indicates, the racial and ethnic homogeneity of arts boards also reflects wider social inequities and discrimination.

Trustees of varied racial and ethnic backgrounds identified the composition of the wider elite as a barrier to greater racial and ethnic diversity. One white trustee said it is hard to find minority candidates because "the likelihood is if they're black . . . they're not going to be very, very rich. The likelihood is that they're also not going to have the potential for raising money." A black trustee wishes his board would cross class lines to achieve more diversity but also believes that class exclusivity is a major barrier to racial and ethnic diversity. He recalled, for instance, meeting someone of Asian descent who he thought would be a good trustee and enhance board diversity but said that she was not a viable candidate. The problem was not her ethnicity—but the fact that "she doesn't have money," and "they don't ask people who can't give to come on the board." As this suggests, to some extent the racial and ethnic exclusivity of the board is a function of its class exclusivity. As noted before, an affluent black donor would be a far more likely candidate than a working-class white person. Still, board ethnic homogeneity cannot be entirely explained as a function of class exclusivity, for these boards have not even successfully identified and recruited those minorities who are available. Rather, the insularity of board culture and networks, ethnic and racial divisions in the wider society, and the willingness and ability of these predominantly white boards to undertake more proactive and time-consuming efforts are also factors.

Boards are self-perpetuating entities who select their own members. When trustees propose possible candidates, they typically look to those who are known within their own social and business networks. And, as one trustee acknowledged, "you tend to know people or hear about people that are similar to you. That's one problem." This process did, for instance, bring on a black and a Hispanic trustee with social and professional ties to current board members. But it is not a process that will identify those who are not already in such networks. It is, for instance, less likely to point trustees toward candidates whose financial success has been achieved outside of white-owned and managed firms.

White trustees repeatedly say that it is hard to find affluent minorities, and even harder to find those who are interested in the institution and willing to contribute. By way of evidence, for instance, they point to the scarcity of minorities in their audience, and their promptness in recruiting those who are participants and donors. Yet what these predominantly white boards apparently have not done is come to a more thorough and accurate understanding of why there is not a greater minority presence both in the ranks of their audience and within the ranks of their donors.

Trustees assume that the lack of participation in their institutions is indicative of a lack of interest on the part of minorities. Yet the results of the Tulip Opera initiative to involve more affluent Hispanics indicates that this assumption is not necessarily accurate. What that most unusual effort uncovered was the fact that there were many affluent Hispanics in the community who were great opera enthusiasts, who listened to opera at home, and who attended operas in other cities. These men and women liked opera very much, but they did not go the opera in their own city. Many explained that they were not comfortable going to a large venue in their own community where they did not know other people, which made them feel like strangers. Although they did not know people at the opera in other cities, this was not experienced in a similar fashion. As one person put it, in another city, one is "a foreigner in a foreign country," a very different feeling than that of being a foreigner in one's own community. Moreover, people expressed a related preference for doing activities such as going to the opera as part of a sociable group. One Hispanic trustee characterized many Americans' nonchalant practice of going to the opera as part of a couple or even alone as "a totally different psychology."

Once understood, however, specific strategies were adopted to address the particular barriers in question. Thus, for instance, the woman who led the initiative organized groups of Hispanics to attend the opera together, and held social events coordinated with performances. Such social events were held at the opera house, so that attendees would become familiar with and feel at home in the venue. In fact, much of her approach essentially involved taking strategies traditionally used to promote identification and involvement among affluent, white patrons, and extend them to a new group, in this case affluent Hispanics. Indeed, over time, people who had started to attend the opera as part of the organized groups started to get together and buy tickets on their own. By the time of the interviews, interest was substantial enough so that a successful fundraiser had been held, and thoughts were turning to enhancing the involvement of Hispanics as volunteers and financial supporters.

In sum, this example shows that, while members of a particular ethnic community may not be involved with an institution in larger numbers, this does not necessarily indicate a lack of interest in the mission of the institution. It also shows, however, that even when such interest does exist, it may well be necessary for the current board to take a proactive and long-term plan to bridge whatever the divide is that exists and to further develop the high level of involvement that current trustees would like to see precede an invitation to the board. The Tulip Opera initiative was not undertaken in the expectation that the Hispanics they approached would immediately donate time or money. But as the effort progressed, this started to become a realistic expectation, and as it continues to grow, it is anticipated that the effort will ultimately contribute to increasing the pool of board candidates. Especially for the highly selective Orchid City institutions, however, it is perhaps more typical for these trustees to assume that people will come to them than to think about convincing people to seek board membership.

To this point, we have seen how misperceptions rooted in cultural and social distance serve as a barrier to diversification. It is also true, however, that negative stereotypes and assumptions in the wider society may perpetuate the idea, at least among some people, that suitable members of minority groups are hard to find. For instance, a Hispanic trustee was discussing a plan to raise funds from affluent Hispanic businesspeople at a luncheon and was overheard by an Anglo woman, who asked, "Hispanics who make three million dollars or more a year—

where did you get that idea?" Said the trustee, "I told her 'Just call the Chamber of Commerce, and ask for Hispanic businesses that make more than $3 million a year, and you'll have it, just as I have it.'"

Conclusion

A central insight of elite theory is that elites must adapt if they and their institutions are to survive.[8] In the face of societal changes and organizational needs, today these boards feel that they must adapt to become more racially and ethnically inclusive. Moreover, trustees say that they want to become more diverse and believe it is the right thing to do. The way that they approach diversity and the limits to their efforts are influenced by current board culture and composition. When these boards set out to become more racially and ethnically inclusive, they still seek to remain within the boundaries of class. Black or white, Hispanic or non-Hispanic, these boards try to recruit those who are affluent and have the types of political, corporate, and social connections enjoyed by members of the elite.

I have argued in this chapter that attention to diversity is prompted by external societal changes and the related perception that doing so is related to the financial and legitimacy needs of the organizations. Thus, in Tulip City, where it is seen as a matter of organizational survival itself, diversity was a major issue in the interviews and characterized as one of the central issues facing the board. This highlights how the perception that diversity is directly related to organizational self-interests influenced the degree of urgency and concern with which it is discussed. But discussing and implementing diversity are two very different matters. It remains an open question as to whether any of the perceptions or motivations that currently inform trustee thinking will be adequate to actually move these boards to take the steps necessary to implement substantial diversity.

Although they say they want diversity, these boards remain racially and ethnically homogeneous. Trustees acknowledge that this is the case but say that it does not reflect a lack of effort on their part. According to them, it is hard to find affluent members of minority groups in general, and particularly ones who are both affluent and interested in the institution. Board homogeneity, they say, reflects the lack of minorities in their audience and support base.

It is true that the homogeneity of elite boards partly reflects larger economic inequities that have impeded greater inclusion of minorities in elite economic positions. Yet as we have seen, these boards have not even been able to recruit many of those affluent and interested minorities who are available. To understand the ongoing homogeneity of these boards thoroughly would require speaking with affluent members of various ethnic communities in these cities to hear their points of view about these institutions, and indeed to see whether they have ever been approached to participate. Yet even without such input, the very facts and observations offered by white trustees serve to undermine their own contention that they are doing all they can.

This raises the question as to whether, despite what they say, trustees really are not willing to admit minorities to the board. Yet the material does not support that conclusion either. These boards have willingly recruited people who become known to them, and those minorities who do serve on the board say they feel welcome. Specific examples can be cited both during and since the time of the interviews in which sizeable financial donations by members of minority groups were followed by inclusion on the board.

In reality, I believe, these boards are not resisting the inclusion of minorities (who fit their class criteria), but neither are they making the level of effort that they claim. They may willingly, even eagerly, recruit those affluent minorities who are already supportive of the institution or who they know through personal contact. They have not, however, successfully gone out, identified, and recruited other people. The very insularity and homogeneity that trustees say they want to overcome hinders their attaining the diversity that they say they seek. As one black trustee said in exasperation, "They say that they can't find people, but the reason is that [when they look] they ask each other." In addition to the insularity of their networks, trustees operate on a series of unfounded assumptions and misperceptions that impede diversity efforts, but whose veracity they do not even question.

A case in point is the assumption that lack of greater participation by minorities indicates lack of interest. Many white trustees think this is true, but it is an unsupported assumption that is directly challenged by evidence. As we have seen, the Tulip Opera initiative found that there were numerous affluent Hispanics with a strong interest in opera. It was true that they were not attending but not because of lack of interest. Once the actual barriers were discovered, they could be addressed, and indeed the initiative has met with success. Yet this example is of such interest because it is so unusual, and the fact that it is so unusual is yet another indication of the fact that these boards are not trying as hard as they could.

It is hard for these boards to find minorities, but trustees do not consider the extent to which their own insularity and faulty assumptions contribute to the difficulty. Moreover, a successful effort like that at the Tulip Opera indicates that to achieve the type of diversity they say they seek will require far more than merely welcoming those interested minorities of whom they become aware. Rather, it will require precisely the type of proactive, focused, and sustained efforts that most of these white trustees are unlikely to be able or willing to devise or implement. Indeed, the very stance of going out to find and convince people to become involved is at odds with the elite character of these boards, more prone to thinking of membership as a coveted honor. In Orchid City particularly, these boards are more accustomed to having people volunteer to give large sums in hopes of inclusion. While saying "no" to some who want to join or "yes" to those ready to make substantial commitments is consistent with trustees' own perceptions about these prestigious boards, going out to solicit interest is not. This is yet another reason why a perception that it is in the organization's self-interest to attract more minorities is a critical spur to inducing more proactive efforts.

Still, trustees clearly react supportively when proactive efforts are made, as in the Tulip Opera case. But their lack of familiarity with the communities in question, the fact that they devote their energies on the board to areas where they do feel a connection, and the fact that efforts such as the Tulip Opera one require a high level of commitment and time, all this makes it unlikely that most white trustees would become personally involved. Indeed, supportive as they are, they are not personally involved in the Tulip Opera effort.

One black trustee said his board cannot do outreach because they have no understanding of minority communities, and his observation has relevance for board diversity. The clear implication is that, just as external prompts have been necessary to focus these boards' attention on diversity, external help is needed for them to achieve it. To this end, it is most significant that when top professional positions needed to be filled recently, both Tulip City boards chose individuals clearly committed to developing relationships with more of the city's diverse ethnic communities. In one case, the appointment went to an individual who is also of the ethnic origins of one of the communities that they seek to involve.

Finally, we must keep in mind that the diversity that these boards seek is diversity within a larger continuity. Not only do they seek others with a comparable class position, but those whose priorities and ways of operating fit within the current board's framework and culture. Particularly in Tulip City, trustees have supported some artistic programming adaptations believed to have the potential to attract more minority participation. Whatever their willingness or enthusiasm though, there is every sign that trustees' support for change with respect to diversity would likely weaken considerably were it to involve fundamental changes to other aspects of the board or the organization. As one Tulip opera trustee, a supporter of recruiting more minorities, said:

> We do our best reaching out, and try to figure out how to get to a broader community, like talking about this Kabuki opera . . . But we're not willing to throw away opera as it was, as it is, a western world invention. We're

not willing to throw it away and say it's so elitist that we want to disengage . . . If we can adapt in some ways, we're going to try to do that. But we're not going to walk away from opera . . . We know that's a tough row here. It's not easy in a community that itself is changing to try to be a last . . . holdout in a western art form. But we're going to try—if we can afford it.

CHAPTER FOUR

Fundraising and the Role of the Elite Board

This chapter extends the book's analysis of the dual influences of class and organization to an examination of how trustees understand and implement their roles. In doing so, the discussion focuses particularly on the board's fundraising role. The prominence of fundraising in this chapter reflects its prominence in the minds of trustees. More than any other role, generating funds was clearly, consistently, and uniformly highlighted as critical by trustees of all four boards. A typical example was a trustee who emphasized that of the board's roles, "fundraising is terribly important. I think it's the most important."

The motivations that bring elites to these boards also influence how they think and act as trustees. Trustees see their role as preserving the organization, its mission, and its identity. As one board member said, "The trustee's responsibility is primarily to look at the good of the particular institution that they're involved with, and keep it going into perpetuity." To accomplish this goal, trustees must address organizational needs, but they do so in ways that reflect a class-related outlook that they bring to the board. The approach taken by these boards to fundraising is a case in point.

Fundraising itself is not unique to elite arts boards, who do assume roles that are also undertaken by other types of boards.

Class, however, influences the particular way in which elite trustees carry out this role. The very way these boards raise money depends on their access to resources and networks that trustees have by virtue of their elite position. The emphasis these boards place on fundraising, moreover, is reinforced by the costliness of their commitment to sustaining these institutions as elite within their fields.

Fundraising does address an organizational need for funds, and, as currently structured, these institutions rely on having access to the resources provided by an elite board. At the same time, the way these boards raise money also serves a function among the elite. The board's importance in raising money among the affluent, and the various social events surrounding fundraising, perpetuate the exclusivity and status of the niche elites establish for themselves in relation to these organizations. Fundraising as carried out on these boards also reinforces board exclusivity, by making wealth and connections virtual prerequisites for performing what trustees define as a central board role.

The board's fundraising role relates to central aspects of board culture and operations, including how trustees define their sphere of authority and that of staff. Trustees regard fundraising as a central board task and believe that they have a unique ability to raise large donations from their wealthy peers. In this respect, fundraising presents a direct contrast to trustees' acceptance of staff expertise and authority in the artistic arena.

In response to heightened financial needs, boards have overseen the professionalization of their organizations' fundraising apparatus and approved measures designed to attract resources from a wider audience. When it comes to raising money among their peers, however, they also preserve a particular role and separate niche for themselves, exhibiting once again the bifurcation that characterizes their basic approach to the institution. Professionals certainly play an important role in fundraising among the affluent, but the board retains a distinctive role for itself that depends on the elite status of its members.

As we shall also see, gender plays a role with respect to how boards carry out their class-related approach to raising funds. Trustees believe that they have a role to play both in raising money and in overseeing the management and use of that money by the organization. The relative likelihood of a trustee's engaging in one or the other roles, however, varies among male and female trustees, as does the particular area of fundraising in which they engage.

In principle, class influences and organizational needs complement one another in the board's fundraising role. As the system is structured, board prestige and exclusivity is put to the service of attracting funds for the institutions. In actuality, however, organizational needs and status-related dimensions of the board can and have come into tension. There is always the risk that the board's emphasis on fundraising, and its social character, may overwhelm, rather than reinforce the board's other governance activities and attention to a wider range of organizational needs.

Certainly with respect to the older Orchid City organizations, the current level of attention to fundraising itself represents a shift within the board. At the time of the study, the Tulip Museum, which had placed comparatively less demands on trustees in this area, had been prompted by financial crisis to make fundraising more central and to expand the array of status-related incentives to attract funds from the wealthy. In the previous chapter, we saw that increased financial needs lead boards to accept greater openness concerning organizational services and programs. The increased emphasis on fundraising also leads to changes within the board itself—not by making the board any less elite, but by influencing the relative importance ascribed to various dimensions of elite position (e.g., money versus social status), and by influencing the types of elite members invited to serve.

"Give, Get, or Get Off": The Centrality of Fundraising

More than any other board role, generating funds through personal donations and/or fundraising was clearly and consistently cited as important by trustees of all four boards.[1] Similarly, the vast majority of trustees on every board believe that the ability to give and/or raise money is an important criterion in a trustee.[2] Trustees even referred to a saying, according to which, an individual should "give, get, or get off" the board.

One trustee who feels that fundraising is the board's most important role said, "you've got [millions of] dollars to raise every year, and everybody should have some part in that." A member of another board believes that "in the end, the main purpose of the board is to raise the money to carry out the organization's activity." A trustee of a third institution feels that the board is supposed "to provide all kinds of resources to management, if you will, but basically it's there to raise money."

When trustees characterized boards as having multiple responsibilities, as many did, generating funds was typically included. For instance, board roles were described as giving time and raising money, hiring management and raising money, ensuring financial accountability and raising money, and setting organizational policy and raising money. The centrality of the board's donative and fundraising role is one important way that trustees distinguish between their responsibilities as members of nonprofit versus corporate boards.

Trustees argue that because of their role in raising money, most board members must either have the personal wealth to contribute, or have connections to wealth. One man said, "Economic survival is number one . . . And this is not callous, but de facto—If people cannot contribute, or are not able to raise substantial money, you really cannot ask them to join the board." A trustee of another board observed, "It is expensive to be part of the board . . . There is a financial responsibility. And we do have one or two trustees who . . . cannot make that kind of commitment, but you can't have more than a few." Similarly, a member of a third board explained that "you need money to run these institutions" and the more wealthy people you involve as trustees, the greater the chance of attracting their contributions.

As we can see, wealth (or connections to wealth) are a virtual prerequisite to fulfilling the trustee role as defined on these boards. The ability to contribute financially was seen as especially necessary to serving in certain board roles. For instance, trustees of both museums characterized their acquisitions committee as a "big bucks" committee, whose members are expected to help acquire new works. One trustee said that acquisitions is "the fun committee"—but only if you have substantial resources. He explained that during meetings, "what they do is, little notes are passed [saying], 'I'll give half, if you'll give half.'" As a member of the committee recalled, when the museum lacked sufficient funds for one purchase, several trustees each "forked out" a (six-figure) donation to make up the balance. An acquisitions committee member at the other museum characterized the committee as a "pressure situation," because a fellow member will offer to donate and then ask others to contribute. He also believes, however, that were these trustees not on the board, the institutions would not be able to raise as much money. This last observation reminds us that one of the elite board's most powerful fundraising tools is inclusion within its ranks.

An emphasis on fundraising reinforces the elite exclusivity of these boards. It can, however, challenge forms of exclusivity that these boards have exercised within the elite. Traditional upper-class boards, for instance, have resisted including members capable of contributing large sums but who are perceived as "outsiders."[3] By using such status-based criteria, however, trustees also exclude individuals who might have greater financial resources to contribute to the institution. Indeed, when financial pressures and concerns about raising money mounted, prestigious boards also opened up their ranks to new, and previously excluded, millionaires, such as Jews.[4]

As we can see, an emphasis on fundraising has consequences for the types of elites recruited to boards, and for the priority assigned to different dimensions of elite status (e.g., wealth versus status-based criteria such as family background). Particularly at the older Orchid City institutions, trustees reported that money had become a more important criterion in board recruitment. Said one long-time member, "Thirty years ago you had people who were not either major contributors or raising money, who were just there because they like opera, and . . . they knew somebody who got them on the board. It's harder to do that today."

Class and Fundraising on Elite Arts Boards

When elite boards engage in fundraising, they respond to an organizational need for funds. The way in which they respond, however, reflects trustees' class-related outlook, and their expectations concerning the stature of the institution. Boards expect members to donate large sums and to raise large sums from their peers. They do this in ways tailored to their elite position, and at a level that enables them to sustain the institutions as elite within their field. Although these boards are budget-conscious, they want the institutions to be run in a way that they believe embodies quality and excellence. They are prepared to raise and spend the amounts needed to accomplish this goal. As one trustee said, "our objective cannot be just to balance the budget. It has to be to provide the best." This is a costly undertaking, and an opera trustee who said, "we can afford to do the productions correctly," also observed that the institution is "an enormous, money-devouring machine."

As is true of many nonprofits, these museums and operas do not generate enough earned income (e.g., through admissions and ticket sales) to cover their expenses. They rely, accordingly, on fundraising to provide additional revenues, and the sums of money needed to fill the gap between expenses and revenues has only increased. Trustees' emphasis on the board's donative and fundraising roles reflects their efforts to meet this organizational need for funds. While there are many reasons for the institutions ever-greater need for funds,[5] trustees' commitment to sustaining and enhancing organizational stature is one contributing factor. With respect to this commitment, the goals of trustees coincide with those of professional staff, who also want the board to raise as much money as possible.[6] Moreover, board and organizational prestige are interconnected, and by maintaining organizational stature, trustees also reinforce the status of the board.

Elite boards raise money at a level that reflects their trustees' elite resources and connections. One Tulip City board, for instance, expected a minimum annual contribution from trustees that was in excess of the median annual earnings of full-time American workers. Still, one board member suspects that another arts institution expects several times that amount. Asked whether he aspires to match that, he said, "you have to." The board of an Orchid City institution refused membership to one wealthy individual, because he refused to increase his annual contributions to a six figure amount. These instances refer to annual giving, but some trustees give major individual donations, which can amount to millions of dollars. For instance, a museum trustee donated a valuable art collection and funds for a gallery. During the interview, she jokingly apologized for the lack of paintings in her apartment, saying that they are now all in the museum.

Trustees raise money in a way that relies on their own ability to contribute funds. One board leader raised money for one undertaking by going to fellow trustees and saying, "I'm going to give $100,000 and I expect you to, too." A trustee on another board successfully adopted a similar strategy, by pledging to contribute a million dollars if a certain number of other people would give the same amount. When selecting a new head for their board, trustees of one institution considered several criteria, including potential candidates' ability to contribute. Explaining their rationale, a member of the selection committee said, "when you have the capacity to be generous, you can speak to other people about being generous. If you can't give yourself . . . [it's] very hard to raise significant amounts from other people."

Boards also raise money by organizing galas and other events that link fundraising to exclusive social occasions among the elite. For instance, one opera raises a great deal by holding a yearly gala, where people attend "in all their finery" and are photographed for the society column. A museum successfully raises money through an event organized around exhibition openings that has become, as one trustee put it, "an important social occasion." A woman who has had great success in raising money believes that "people will pay any price to come" to an event, provided that it is well organized, done in "good taste," and targets the "right people."

The high cost of such events keeps them exclusive, and also reinforces the exclusivity of the board. As board members themselves observed, the obligation to attend such events, makes trusteeship expensive even apart from the expected donations. Indeed, an unusual trustee who advocated opening the board to more people of lesser means said that one of the steps that would have to be taken would be to underwrite the costs of attendance. He also said, however, that there was little support among the rest of the board for seeking out those unable to contribute financially for membership.

Trustees employ other strategies they feel will respond to the interests and preferences of their peers. Some board members have private receptions and dinners in their own elegant homes and entertain wealthy potential donors in other prestigious settings. For instance, one board initially approached a very wealthy woman they wanted to involve further by having a trustee invite her and her husband to dinner and then to a private and exclusive venue at the institution. She accepted the invitation and has since become a member of the board.

Trustees provide affluent donors with personal attention and recognition for their donations. To honor a major contributor, one board held a lavish dinner with a prestigious guest list that received coverage in the newspaper. An officer of another board regularly sends handwritten, personal notes to large donors. When he became an officer, "they sent me all this stationery. I figured, hell, what do I need all of this stationery? I found out."

Class, Fundraising, and Board Authority

By virtue of their own class position, trustees believe that they have a distinctive expertise when it comes to raising money among their affluent peers. Said one woman, "People who give that much money are looking for different kinds of things." Trustees believe that they know how to provide those things and tailor their approach to the lifestyle and interests of their peers. Trustees view fundraising for these large institutions as a major undertaking requiring multiple participants and have endorsed the expansion and professionalization of fundraising within these institutions. Yet they also believe that the board retains an important fundraising role that cannot be duplicated by professional staff.

Said one opera trustee, "a staff can organize things, and even locate people from whom to fundraise, but to fundraise itself you need the board." She went on to explain, "People give . . . when they're asked directly, and they give when they are asked by a peer." Similarly, a museum trustee believes that "fundraising can't be done without the board," because "the donor wants to talk to a board member, not to a paid development person." Such comments not only reflect trustees' class-based approach to raising money, but also the status distinctions that they draw between themselves and professional staff, regardless of how highly admired.

As we can see, trustees' approach to fundraising relies not only on the involvement of the board, but on involvement of a *prestigious* board. Elites raise money through their personal networks but also use board and trustee prestige to attract other wealthy people to the organization and its events. This point is underscored by a comparison that one trustee (and member of both) drew between the fundraising capabilities of the institution's own board and the board of its support institution. The board, she explained, can reach "the blue ribbon social strata." By contrast, the support organization's board proved unable to do certain fundraising events because, "it didn't have that level of cachet. Big donors want that."

Trustees' outlook concerning the board's fundraising role is illustrated by a disagreement that arose between one opera's board and staff. The board planned a fundraising gala around the opening night of the opera. Professional staff chose the opera to be performed. Trustees, however, objected to the choice, saying that the long length of the opera would interfere with the social nature of the evening. They complained that "dinner would've started at one in the morning," and that "for an opening night performance, people don't want it to be an overnight." One trustee said that the professional who chose the opera just doesn't understand the "social raising of money." The board prevailed, and a shorter and more popular piece was selected.

Trustees do not define opening night as an artistic occasion, but as a fundraising and social occasion, and therefore within their domain. Thus, although they defer to this professional's artistic authority and expertise on other occasions, they challenged his decision in this situation. Not only was the administrator unsuccessful, he reinforced doubts trustees already had about his financial acumen and left the board feeling more justified about intervening in financial management. This example further highlights the links between fundraising, organizational needs, and class status that are made in trustees' approach to raising money. The opening night event raises a lot of money, and trustees argued that its social character had to be maintained for the financial good of the organization. Yet at the same time that the board protected the "social raising of money" on behalf of the institution, they were also protecting a prestigious social event that attracts their peers and forms part of the exclusive niche in which elites interact with one another and these organizations.

Class, Gender, and the Financial Role of the Board

Class shapes the board's approach to fundraising, but gender also comes into play with respect to how trustees involve themselves in this role. Gender differences exist not only in the area of raising money but also in board oversight of the institution's financial resources. Women were more likely than men to serve on a board committee related to fundraising, but men were more likely to be on committees concerned with overseeing the use and management of financial resources. The percentage of women serving on a development-related committee (45.8) was over twice as high as the percentage of men (20.4). By contrast, the percentage of men serving on a finance-related committee (such as budget, investment, finance) was almost three times as high (36.7) as the percentage of women (12.5).[7] On one board, two out of three finance-related committees included no women at all. These differences reflect wider traditional upper-class gender divisions, including men's involvement in economic areas and women's involvement in the social dimensions of the life of their class.[8]

Fundraising is an activity that is engaged in by men and

women, including those who are not specifically members of development committees. Male trustees actively raise money and also have a considerable presence on such development-related committees. Women are, however, particularly identified with "special events," or the types of social fundraising events discussed earlier. A businesswoman who is on a finance-related committee said it was "very unusual" for a woman to sit on that committee. She said, "they are more usually involved in the social aspect. We have several women who are very, very good at that . . . That happens not to be my specialty."

Women's involvement in organizing special events parallels their role in coordinating the social dimensions of upper class life. By contrast, men's predominance on finance-related committees reflects their involvement in business (and upper class women's traditional distance from the business world). A woman who does not work, and who is active in special events, said, "You need businesspeople for a lot of things like [the] investment committee. That wouldn't be something I would or could do. Sometimes we do have women from the financial world who get involved with those things." A woman who does serve on her board's finance committee said that to be a member you should have a background in finance, but "most women don't." One unusual woman, though, already an active trustee, specifically asked to join the budget committee because "they really do fight out a lot of policy there . . . I thought it was time for the women to have something besides the soft committees."

Women's fundraising activities have in the past been overlooked or stereotyped as somewhat frivolous.[9] Perhaps because of the central role of fundraising on these boards today, however, men and women were cognizant of the importance of special events and women felt that their activities were appreciated. Indeed, a female trustee recognized for her talents in raising funds and organizing special events was named as an officer of the board shortly after the time of the study. Women who have been active in other areas of development also are among their boards' influential trustees. For instance, a woman who helped found an advisory body whose members contribute substantially to the institution is an officer of her board.

The changing nature of gender roles, however, poses as yet unanswerable but important questions. The types of events traditionally organized by women are a critical element of sustaining the social aspects and prestige of elite involvement with the institutions. A major question, however, is whether women will continue to be as available for that role in the future, as they increasingly do move into the business world. One businesswoman, for instance, even hesitated to describe what she does on the board as fundraising, although she is on a development committee, because, "That can connote the notion that I'm involved in some way in special events or social reach out. I do none of that. I have no skills at it . . . I'm not interested in it . . . It's more the business side that I'm involved in." Future shifts in the role of women on boards, and the consequences for elite fundraising, cannot be predicted at this point, when the overwhelming majority of women are in traditional roles. What does seem likely is that women will increasingly be seen in financial oversight roles traditionally held by men. To what extent businesswomen will join these boards, and the consequences of women's role in fundraising, however, remains to be seen. Given women's importance in the ongoing maintenance of the prestige used to attract donations, however, it is an issue of potentially major significance for these boards and their institutions. Ironically, were women to withdraw from their traditional fundraising roles, they would do so at a time when their activities, traditionally viewed with a certain amount of condescension, as frivolous, have come to be recognized as central within the board's fundraising focus.

Given that business skills are seen as central for membership on board committees of major importance, the future occupational background women bring to trusteeship also has a bearing on women's access to influential board roles. The degree of women's access to major board roles is a complicated and mixed one. When asked, women repeatedly said that their boards had no "glass ceiling." Yet the top officers (chair, president) of all four boards were men, and women's absence from financial oversight committees puts them at a distance from a major area of board influence. Still, women have occupied the top officer positions on two of the four boards in the past, and they currently occupied other officer positions (such as vice-president) on two boards. The composition of the influential executive committee also presents a mixed picture of women's access to influential positions. Female trustees were less likely to be on one board's executive committee, but gender did not influence executive committee membership on the two other boards with such a committee.[10] Women were a strong presence on both museum acquisitions committees, certainly among the important and desirable board committees.

Although women clearly do achieve influence, and sometimes are among the most influential trustees, their distance from the business world does delimit that influence, particularly as boards increasingly approach these institutions as complex businesses. As women increasingly come to the board with a financial background, however, that is a limitation that may also diminish.

Class, Organizational Needs, and Board Roles

Board roles and the relative emphasis given to board roles, are not static.[11] Rather, they change in ways that are influenced by shifting organizational circumstances and by changes within the elite. This was reflected in variations that exist between the boards, as well as changes within individual boards over time. Indeed, at the time of the study, the Tulip Museum, in the wake of a series of crises was in the process of actively restructuring and revising the board's role.

All four boards share an emphasis on giving and raising money, but they also exhibit differences related to their particular circumstances. All trustees would agree that hiring top professional staff is a major board responsibility, but only at the Tulip Museum were trustees currently focusing on that role, because the institution was seeking a new director. Given the circumstances, trustees had also taken on certain managerial roles that would normally be handled by the director. To take another example, only at the comparatively young Tulip Opera did trustees (just over one-fourth) identify generating community awareness and support for the organization as a board role. At the museums, which receive substantial local government funding, some trustees play a role in institutional dealings with government. Yet even when the individual roles or focus may vary, all four boards still exhibit a commonality in that they approach these in a way that is rooted in their class. For instance, Tulip Opera trustees try to "get the word out" by bringing wealthy acquaintances to performances. Similarly, museum boards include trustees whose elite standing facilitates access to politicians when the board wants to air their point of view.

The board's role in fundraising, as well as in overseeing other ventures intended to raise money for the institution, is also subject to change. This is seen in the older Orchid City institutions. Trustees of these organizations have always had an important donative role, and indeed their contributions were instrumental in founding the organizations. An early chair of one institution readily solved the problem of a deficit in funds at the end of the year, by having trustees contribute the balance. Yet as the organizations and their financial needs grew, so too did the organization's fundraising apparatus and the board's donative and fundraising role. Board efforts to increase organizational funds through retailing activities also creates new board roles. Thus, the Orchid Museum established a committee to oversee these activities, while the operas have brought on trustees who they felt would be helpful in creating media opportunities and connections for their organizations.

A major theme on these boards is the increasingly business-like character of the institutions. Many trustees likened their organization's finances to those of a complex business, and this has consequences for the board's role. Said one trustee, "It's a business, and runs like a business, and has the needs of a business." This is illustrated, for instance, in the evolution of the Orchid Museum's committee structure. As the institution grew in size and complexity, the number of board committees almost doubled in size, with new and more differentiated finance-related committees established. Instead of a single finance committee, the board now had multiple finance-related committees,

including not only finance, but investment, and audit committees. Indeed, one reason that boards recruit some people of
comparatively lesser wealth, such as those in top corporate positions, is because they have business skills viewed as relevant for
these committees. One example is a recently retired businessman and member of the Tulip Opera board. Although he is not
in a position to be a large donor, he chairs a financial committee and spends considerable time on organizational finances. As
board roles evolved at the Orchid City institutions, so too did
the variety of elites recruited, which expanded out from the
more traditional upper-class group, becoming more diverse
with respect to religion, family background, and occupation.

At the time of the interviews, the Tulip Museum board
was in the process of a transition that included making board
roles more specific and explicit, with a greater emphasis on raising money. The development reflected in part a financial crisis
caused by a cut in government funding, that, even once resolved,
made it clear that the board and private donors would have to
play a more expanded role. Indeed the institution was subject
to considerable criticism over the board's failure to contribute
more money. Defending themselves, board members point
out that they have donated enormous sums toward construc-
tion and very valuable art collections. Still, with varying degrees
of explicitness, their comments acknowledge that the board
had exhibited weaknesses in carrying out their roles. Said one
trustee, "crisis is great" because it led to rethinking trustee roles,
so that "once your back is against the wall, it creates an odd kind
of opportunity." Said another, "The financial problems made
the board dig in to their own pockets more."

Whereas trustees were formerly recruited without being told

what was expected of them, they are now told explicitly about trustee responsibilities, including the responsibility to provide unrestricted funds annually for operating expenses—in addition to any other donations. One trustee said,

> Now, before we even ask someone to be a trustee, we explain what the obligations are . . . And therefore the culture has changed to the extent that every board member coming on now, and the vast majority of those on the board now, understand that it is part of being a trustee that you contribute, not only to the special things you love and that are fun to give to, but to the ongoing maintenance of the museum, which is what the annual giving campaign is about.

Interestingly, as part of this increased emphasis on the board's financial responsibility, the board also sought to remedy what was perceived as a deficit in their approach and strategy toward donors. A special committee was established to address how greater attention and rewards could be given to large donors.

In terms of the discussion in this chapter, this was a board that had been exclusive but which had not been fully putting its elite character at the service of raising money for the organization. Indeed, an ongoing threat, from an organizational point of view, is that the exchange between elites and the organizations will break down, so that elites maintain board seats without the requirement that they donate. According to the logic of the system in which these boards operate, a board that retains a very wealthy person who does not contribute substantially, is not a properly functioning board. Thus, a trustee approvingly recalled a case in which her board denied membership to a wealthy man because he refused to increase his contributions. She approved because when someone, "want[s] to be on the board, and can afford it, that to me is not right."

Conclusion

Trustees' approach to fundraising, a central emphasis on these boards, shows how elite boards take a role and carry it out in a way that is shaped by class. As we have also seen, gender influences the way in which they implement their roles within this broader class framework. Trustees respond to organizational needs, but their perception of those needs and the nature of their response are guided by the outlook that they bring to the board. One implication is that elite trustees will perceive and respond more readily to organizational needs that they can address in ways that fit more comfortably with their social, cultural, and economic world. As we have seen, trustees define and carry out their role in generating funds in a way that achieves a very close fit indeed. Many trustees own and run businesses, and thus financial oversight is also an area in which they are comfortable and believe they can make a contribution. For instance, one man said that in addition to making donations, he can best serve his museum by volunteering the business skills that have brought him his "good living." Another trustee observed, "we have guys who would charge me an arm and a leg to manage my personal portfolio, and they're managing [the organization's] portfolio. But that's the great thing about the country . . . This great spirit in America of community."

By contrast, however, trustees are less likely to focus on board roles that are more distant from their interests and experiences as elites. This is illustrated by the approach of the board to educational oversight at one museum. Trustees concur that educational activities are part of the institution's central mission, but few board members' major personal interests are in that aspect of the organization. Interestingly, those who do focus on education characterize a part of their role as serving as advocates to the rest of the board, by raising the profile of education and ensuring its place on the board's agenda. For instance, a trustee who believes that education is "what it's all about" successfully worked to have the head of the education department make regular presentations at board meetings. Another trustee whose main interest is in education, said, "I think everybody would say education is important. But I think when it comes down to it . . . there's a tremendous interest in the collection, and that that's a very competing priority . . . No one would ever not vote for something for education. I think that it just needs to be brought to people's attention." Indeed, current board policy was to place greater emphasis on the educational mission of the organization. Still, this does not ensure that trustees in general will pay more attention to it personally, which means that the board may not adequately fulfill its oversight function in an area of major importance.

The importance placed on education, however, is also not static and is subject to change. In Tulip City, where trustees believe that expanding audiences is a matter of organizational survival, educational programs were very much on their mind, and some trustees had made major donations to support efforts in that area. One outcome of the series of crises at the Tulip Museum was a reconsideration of the institution's mission, resulting in a greater emphasis on education. This heightened focus was reflected when the board hired someone with a particular commitment in that area as the institution's professional director.

Elite boards act as a bridge between these prestigious institutions and members of their class, and their networks make them valuable links to the wealthy, the business community, and even the political establishment. Yet this same elite status leaves them poorly positioned to serve as a bridge between the organization and wide segments of the community who are outside of their class. From an organizational perspective, there is always the danger that because of their homogeneity and insularity, these boards will not readily identify certain problems or be prepared to adapt, particularly when doing so requires that they deviate from their characteristic way of functioning. Indeed, it is an open question as to just how much change elite trustees would endorse, in either the institution or the board, without abandoning their support.

The emphasis on the donative and fundraising role of the board reinforces a culture of wealth that suffuses these boards. In principle, the elite culture of the board is supposed to work to the financial benefit of the institution, and indeed it does in certain ways. At the same time, however, there is always the danger that the status culture of the board will conflict with its governance duties and that fundraising will become detached from the board's wider array of responsibilities. The balance between organizational and class influences is negotiated on an ongoing basis within the ranks of these boards and shapes their ongoing culture and evolution, a subject to which we now turn.

CHAPTER FIVE

Status and Governance:
A Delicate Balance

Speaking of an elite board, one trustee said, "It has to have that social cachet, but it has to be kept in bounds." This comment reflects the delicate balance that elite boards must achieve between class-based influences and organizational concerns. As currently structured, these institutions depend on having access to the economic, social, and political resources provided by their elite boards. Board prestige and exclusivity are among the important factors that attract elites. Yet there is always the risk that the status-related aspects of boards will overwhelm, rather than further, their oversight and governance functions.

This chapter examines board culture and organization in relation to the interplay of class and organization. While each board has an individual character, all four have striking similarities in culture and functioning that reflect their common need to respond to, and balance, these dual influences. Indeed, many shifts in boards' structure, and typical challenges that they face, are connected to their ability to balance their status-related role, and attraction to large donors, with their other oversight functions.

All four of these boards display what might be called a culture of excellence. Boards of many types, of course, want their organizations to excel, but elite boards want and expect their institutions to represent, and to be acknowledged as, "the best" in their field. Institutional stature enhances the stature of the board itself, and part of trustees' willingness to mobilize resources for the organization is their desire to associate themselves with, and support, organizations they see as representing the height of excellence. As one opera trustee said, he believes his institution represents "the best," and "a lot of other people" think so too. There are many other companies, he said, "but they just don't have the funds or the facilities." Trustees' emphasis on excellence (as they define it) reinforces the distinctively elite character of the board's culture.

As we have seen, elites carve out a distinctive niche for themselves in relation to these institutions, even as the institutions themselves may become more open and change. While others may use the organizations, elite involvement is carried out separately. The board's centrality to that niche enhances the status of membership. It also heightens trustees' sense of identification with, and responsibility for, the institutions. Trusteeship, in short, represents membership in a select group who enjoy a special association with a well-known and respected institution. In effect, board exclusivity, and elites' distinctive relationship with these prestigious institutions, is among the rewards that they receive in exchange for their financial support.

Board culture and organization is deeply shaped by the centrality that trustees assign to their donative role, which is reinforced by the enormous expense of maintaining these institutions in accordance with their expectations. For many active trustees, financial donations are part of an overall involvement and commitment to the institution. All four boards, however, also include individuals who contribute large sums, but whose other participation is erratic, minimal, or, in certain cases, virtually nonexistent. Finding a way to accommodate such individuals, which boards typically feel they must, while ensuring that an active core is handling the board's oversight functions poses an important challenge. Indeed, to ensure that such functions are carried out, some less wealthy individuals who have certain skills are included, and even attain influence, within the board. Thus, we see again that the elite board must achieve and maintain a delicate balance, in this case between their fundraising and governance activities.

Being "the Best": The Culture of Excellence on Elite Boards

Elite trustees want these institutions to function at the highest level of excellence and to be recognized as representing the best in their fields. This is a factor in their motivations for associating with the organization, for their fundraising efforts, and for their decisions concerning organizational policy. Moreover, the status of the board is connected to the prestige and reputation of the institution. Indeed, budget-minded trustees will opt for a more expensive course of action when they believe that doing so is vital to enhancing and/or maintaining organizational stature.

Trustees repeatedly emphasized the importance of being "the best" and "world class," as well as the importance of organizational stature in attracting the involvement of affluent supporters. A Tulip Museum trustee, for instance, said that one reason he serves is that it is a "dominant" institution, and, "If I'm gonna give my time . . . I . . . want to be giving it to a significant organization." A counterpart in Orchid City similarly said, "most people feel that [this] is an institution of excellence and like to be associated with it. To get their names on something." And one opera trustee succinctly explained that his board wants the institution to be "preeminent . . . and that's what we expect."

The reaction to a cost-saving proposal made by one opera trustee illustrates well the board's emphasis on organizational excellence. After joining the board, this man was surprised to learn just how expensive it is to mount fully staged opera. He suggested that to reduce costs, "maybe we should just dress people up in a tux and let them sing." His fellow trustees, however, just laughed at his suggestion and dismissed his idea as unthinkable—which to them it was. They would rather expend the effort and raise the large sums of money needed to present opera in the way that they feel it should be presented. Indeed, one trustee said that her city should either have a great opera, or none at all. When soaring art prices constrained one of the museum's ability to acquire new works, the board responded with a policy: The institution would continue to acquire only the "highest quality" works even if it meant acquiring less art. The board firmly rejected the option of acquiring even second-rank work in order to make a greater number of acquisitions.

By understanding his board's desire for institutional preeminence, a professional staff member who had a disagreement with the board was able to sway some powerful trustees. The board did not share this professional's desire to present more innovative operas. The disagreement is a common one, that pits the aesthetic goals of arts professionals against the financial orientation of trustees. Trustees objected to innovative operas because they do not sell as well at the box office. In addition, such operas are personally disliked by many trustees.[1]

Rather than try to convince the board on artistic grounds, the professional appealed to their concern for institutional stature. He argued that to be a great opera and attract the best singers, they must include some innovative operas and new productions, despite the high costs. One trustee, who formerly opposed doing innovative operas that only "the avant people like" said he changed his mind after the professional convinced him that, "We wouldn't be a number one opera company if that's what we did . . . Just do the old warhorses, and people look at you like that. You have to do these avant things . . . although they're expensive and money losers, as a part of advancing the art and showing that you can do things." Another trustee, unusual in that he always supported the professional's position, observed that this board has become more receptive to innovation. He linked this shift to the board's concern for organizational stature, when he attributed it to their "experience of the success." Said he, "when we do something a little provocative, critics come in from around the world . . . Also . . . our members have become much more knowledgeable about opera . . . and they're willing to stretch that much further."

Organizational Stature and Civic Pride in Tulip City

In Tulip City, trustees tied the importance of having "world class" institutions to civic stature. They portrayed the (more recent) cultural development of the city as integral to its development as a recognized major urban center. Said one Tulip City resident, "Every major city in the world has [a] performing arts center. And if you're going to be a major city, then you have to have the same thing." Similarly, another said, "This city is becoming a metropolis . . . and I cannot envision that you can have a citadel without the appropriate cultural institutions." Whereas Orchid City trustees are involved with major institutions that have a long and prestigious history, Tulip City trustees see themselves as part of a more recent evolution in their city.

Tulip City trustees expressed dismay at comparisons between their city and other cities with older and more established arts institutions. For instance, one man gets "somewhat defensive" when speaking with people from Orchid City. One reason he joined the board was his desire to bring culture to a "cow town," which he also described as "a city I dearly love." Many Tulip City trustees made reference to a longstanding rivalry with another city in the region, seen as more developed and cosmopolitan. One Tulip City native recalled, "When I was growing up [that city] was always thrown out as a *real* city, and Tulip City was, you know . . . trying to be something, but really wasn't." Tulip City trustees acknowledge their rival's historical preeminence in the arts, but proudly point to the diminishing gap between the two cities. Thus, one trustee confidently predicted that despite their rival's feeling of "superiority," Tulip City is "gaining on them" and "will surpass" them.

The desire to help their city become a recognized, world-class city is among the motivations that have led Tulip City trustees to found and support these institutions. They regard the development of strong arts institutions as a sign of the city's greater maturity and cosmopolitanism. For instance, a man who believes that Tulip City "is going to be one of the number one cities very, very shortly," characterized the increasing activity in the arts as "a natural progression," that occurred as "citizens realize you have to have something more." Another similarly attributed the burgeoning arts organizations as the reflection of the "maturation" of citizens who have "made enough money" and who now "know what institutions are necessary for a city to call itself great." Then again, he added, "on a more parochial level it's . . . the old rivalry with [another city in the region]."

Orchid City trustees also care about the stature of their city's cultural life and believe that great arts institutions are integral to a great city. These trustees, however, already feel confident of their organizations' stature and their city's reputation as, to quote one, "a great repository for culture." [2] Yet Orchid City did not always have such institutions and self-confidence. In the nineteenth century, Orchid City elites sought to create institutions that would rival those of European cities, just as contemporary Tulip City elites compare their city to other, more established American cities. The fact that they do testifies to the ongoing prestige of the arts in the eyes of affluent citizens.

As we see in other areas, the way that Tulip City trustees exercise their sense of civic pride and their aspirations for the community reflects their status as elites. They want to live in a community that can assume a place in the ranks of recognized, world-class cities, and to achieve that end, they prioritize the development of prestigious, fine arts institutions that are valued by their peers. Other members of the community might prioritize different types of institutions, and indeed Tulip City trustees themselves feel they operate in an environment without a strong tradition of cultural philanthropy. Tulip City trustees do endorse measures that they believe will make the institution more attractive to more members of the community, but in the end, their goal is to build and sustain arts institutions that meet their view of excellence and thus contribute to the vision of excellence that they have for their community.

Elites, Excellence, and the Culture of Growth

Trustees connect organizational stature to organizational size. The point is well illustrated by one man, who attributes his institution's prestige to the fact that, "it's richer, it's bigger, and it's better known." Trustees' vision of organizational prestige also promotes what one characterized as the "culture of accumulating money" at elite boards and institutions. One consequence of the connection that trustees draw between organizational prestige and organizational size is that trustees become advocates of growth. Thus, trustees' own policies have contributed to the very heightened financial needs that have prompted boards to become more open with respect to the organizations and their services. Yet by augmenting organizational stature, those same measures have also enhanced the prestige that characterizes the board, and that attracts affluent donors who want to be involved with major institutions.

At various points, all four of these institutions had faced crossroads in which they chose expansion and the goal of organizational preeminence. The Tulip Museum, for instance, evolved out of another institution from which it separated, because, as one trustee put it, they "wanted to be a first rate art museum, and there just wasn't enough space." Confronted with severe financial difficulties, the board of the Orchid Opera rejected the option of scaling back their aspirations and operating in a more limited fashion. Instead, they chose to pursue a policy of aggressive expansion as a way of enhancing revenue. To facilitate that goal the board itself was restructured and became more focused on raising money.

At the time of the study, the Tulip Opera was at an institutional turning point. Changing circumstances involving their performance site provided the opera with an opportunity to consider substantial expansion. Having weathered substantial financial difficulties, trustees on this board are very mindful of containing expenses. Still, notwithstanding the costs entailed, trustees chose a plan of expansion because they wanted to take the institution to yet a higher level of performance. One trustee explained, "We have an opportunity . . . The real challenge now is . . . how do we step up to becoming the great opera company that we could be . . . That includes more opera, higher cost[s]." As we again can see, these trustees seek not only organizational survival but survival at the highest possible level of excellence. As an opera trustee said, "the board is pretty ambitious."

The "ambition" of the board is also seen in the case of museums. Museums in both cities have undergone costly expansion and renovation to their buildings. Said one trustee, "all of these institutions have an unquenchable thirst for money because they are all doing too much . . . All of these institutions build all the time." After saying that his opposition to such projects is atypical, even this trustee qualified his comments by adding that, "if you can show things better [by building], it's important." In the case of one museum, trustees were publicly criticized for overextending the institution through an expensive building program. Board members defended their decision by arguing that they were maintaining the institution's stature, which was critical to attracting donations from top collectors, who would otherwise give their art to other institutions.

Organizational Stature, Trustee Authority, and Professional Staff

Trustees believe that to have organizations of excellence, they must also have professionals who represent the best in their field. They recognize, however, that such individuals also insist on autonomy and authority within their professional domain. As one trustee said, "A great museum has great curators." For this reason, trustees are willing to cede a certain degree of authority to professionals, even where they might prefer to do otherwise.

We have already seen how one opera administrator used trustees' desire for organizational stature to persuade them of the necessity of presenting some innovative operas. Sometimes, trustees defer to staff preferences even when they remain unconvinced, because they feel that overall, staff are achieving their goals of organizational excellence. A case in point is the chair of a board committee, who has been frustrated by what he perceives as staff resistance to greater trustee participation. Although staff keep trustees well-informed, he said, they do so "without any real expectation or wish for comment." He has abandoned what he feels are good ideas for the committee because they met with staff resistance. Nonetheless, he continues to chair the committee and defers to the professionals' wishes, because, "we get informed, and the staff is doing a superb job." [3]

Trustees of another institution are committed to retaining the institution's professional director, even though they are critical of his financial management skills, because "he's been a star, and is the reason we are a world-class [organization]." Indeed, after complaining at length about the director, one trustee said, "On the other hand, if I had to vote tomorrow on whether to [renew] his contract, I would vote in favor." The reason, he explained, is that he credits the director entirely with the institution's stature. As this shows, trustees will even knowingly tolerate, and work around, a perceived major weakness in a professional staff member who is seen as critical to organizational preeminence.

Trustees' willingness to sacrifice a measure of authority in order to retain top professionals is most clearly evidenced in the area of artistic authority. At one opera, for instance, it was particularly clear that trustees wished to have more of a say in artistic matters. The professional director is emphatically opposed, however, and trustees accept his stance as a price they must pay to retain a world-class professional. As one trustee said, "I would like to see the board more involved with the selection of repertory, but that's pretty difficult to do . . . Nobody can ever tell [an accomplished artistic director] what he's going to do." Similarly, a museum acquisitions committee member said, "You look at your strong, respected museum directors . . . They are strong-willed individuals with individual taste, with a respected eye, and they generally guide the choice."

Although trustees defer to professional expertise in artistic matters, their conception of organizational excellence sets the boundaries in which professional staff must function. The board hires and fires the top professional staff, and it is most unlikely that trustees would retain someone who strayed too far from the board's basic vision for the institution. Boards may defer to professional authority, even at times they might prefer to do otherwise—but they do so because of their conviction that overall, professional staff pursue and accomplish goals consistent with their basic values and goals for the institution.

Status, Fundraising, and Organizational Governance

Board and staff are committed to a very costly vision of organizational preeminence. As one trustee said, his institution is "an enormous money-devouring machine." Although these arts institutions are among the wealthiest in the country, trustees often speak as if their very survival were in question. This incongruity partly reflects the board's perspective, in which "survival" means survival at the highest level of stature. From this perspective, the institution's financial needs are the level of resources needed to function at that level.

Trustees' expectations contribute to their emphasis on fundraising and on recruiting board members who have the ability to "give or get" large donations. Board status, in turn, is used to attract the large donations that trustees believe are critical to the success of the organization. Yet boards also have other, governance, duties that are critical to organizational success. The challenge that arises for trustees, however, is that the imperatives of their fundraising role can come into tension with other duties. Accordingly, there is always the danger that fundraising activities will undermine or overwhelm the board's attention to other responsibilities. Yet inadequate attention to fundraising also carries a risk that trustees will not fulfill a role they have assumed and upon which the institutions depend.

Board size exemplifies how fundraising-related criteria can come into tension with other, governance-related considerations. All four of these boards are fairly large, as is characteristic of many nonprofit institutions.[4] Even the smallest had close to thirty members at the time of the interviews, and usually is somewhat larger in size. Large boards are advantageous from a fundraising perspective, because seats can be used to attract and reward generous donors. Yet large boards are unwieldy and therefore problematic from a governance perspective. Trustees often observed, for instance, that the board's large size precludes genuine discussions during meetings. Said one, "Ideally, the board would be smaller, but because fundraising is a major function, you have a large one."[5]

Boards try to achieve a size that balances these competing considerations. Toward that end, they occasionally make adjustments in board size. For instance, the smallest of the four boards reduced its size considerably as part of an extensive board reorganization. A long-time trustee recalled, "It was just so big it was unwieldy." A reduction in size was being contemplated on the largest board for similar reasons, a change that has been made since the time of the interviews. On a third board, comparable problems arose with respect to the size of the executive committee. In addition to having a large board, in this case the executive committee had become a "prestige committee" that was too large to function effectively. Prompted by a financial crisis, the board reorganized to strengthen its operations and reduced the size of the committee.

The very prestige of the board is a double-edged sword because donors who are not asked to join may be insulted and reduce or withhold donations. As the head of one nominating committee explained,

> We have to be careful. There are people who are enormously involved with the institution, generous to it. And we have to make clear it's no sign of lack of appreciation . . . that they're not invited to come on the board, because the composition of the board at any given time is a function of needing different strengths.

In response to the tensions between fundraising and governance imperatives, boards seek to develop alternatives to trusteeship in order to recognize a larger number of donors. One example is the use of an "honorary" trustee category. One trustee, for instance, said his board increasingly uses this category as a way to say "thank you" to important contributors that are not seen as appropriate for the board. Additional alternatives include the creation of other formal bodies, such as advisory boards, that can incorporate additional donors and may exceed the size of the board. One trustee characterized these bodies as "masks," whose real function is to raise money for the organizations. Such bodies are fundraising tools, but they are also used to serve other purposes. One board, for instance, uses an advisory body as a training ground for future members. Trustees hope that by first serving on other associated bodies, individuals will not only develop a willingness to donate money, but also the interest and experience needed to eventually assume the wider range of trustee responsibilities.

Whatever alternative mechanisms they may use, all four boards include major donors who do not actively participate in other board activities and feel that such individuals should be accommodated. One trustee, for instance, believes her board is right to retain certain members who do not attend meetings but give money and "like to see their name listed as a director." Asked why they should be retained, she promptly replied that they would not contribute were they not trustees. Similarly, a member of another board supports retaining one member who has *never* attended a meeting, because he "gives a very nice gift, and if you need something, some strings pulled someplace, he can pull them."

As this discussion suggests, individuals able to fulfill the board's donative role are not necessarily most able or willing to assume other board responsibilities. Therefore, tensions between fundraising and governance-related criteria can also arise when boards recruit new members. Nominating committee members say that they try to achieve a "balanced" composition that will allow the board to fill a range of fundraising and other oversight duties. As noted earlier, for instance, boards appoint some (relatively) less affluent individuals who have valued business skills. Referring to one such individual, a nominating committee member said, "He gives an enormous amount . . . There are places for various skills." Still, the numbers of less affluent members are limited, and boards certainly prioritize those able to make large donations. Given the enormous emphasis on fundraising and the prestige associated with trusteeship, there is considerable pressure on these boards to offer open seats to major donors on the basis of their ability to contribute.

Boards also have a considerable incentive to retain those trustees who do contribute generously. Their interest in doing so can produce tensions when boards also decide that turnover is important to strengthen the board. Ironically, the only board that had term limits also had the longest average years of service among trustees. This museum board's term-limit policy is designed to encourage turnover but allows for exceptions in the case of particularly valued members, including those who are important donors. For instance, one active trustee said that he was retained beyond the limit because the board did not want to lose him or the art collection he will donate to the organization. Another institution sets an age limit for members, also a policy designed to encourage turnover. In many cases, though, the retirement of an important trustee is followed by the appointment of a spouse (usually a younger wife) or child. In one case, people actually continued to speak of a major donor as if he were still on the board, although he had retired and been replaced by his wife. These cases show again how fundraising considerations can come into tension with other governance considerations, in this case, trustees' belief that it is important to infuse the board with new faces.

To this point, I have focused on the potential disparity between those able to further the board's fundraising and other governance goals. A further risk faced by these boards, though, is that someone they do recruit because of their financial resources will then fail to contribute either time or money. Such an individual may want the status associated with trusteeship, yet be unwilling "to pay," to quote one trustee. According to the logic of the system in which these boards operate, a board that admits a wealthy member who does not substantially contribute, is a poorly functioning board.

Furthermore, there is always the chance that a donor's individual agenda will not coincide with perceived organizational needs and priorities as seen by the board and staff. Although disagreements between donors and recipient institutions are not uncommon, the situation is especially problematic when the donor is also a trustee. In such cases, conflict can be brought into the board itself, and questions may arise about the trustee's commitment to serving the good of the organization. Both museums, for instance, experienced conflicts when collectors on the board were unwilling to donate art without restrictions that were seen as onerous by other trustees and professional staff. At one institution, trustees did contribute large sums for purposes they found personally rewarding but not necessarily for other important institutional needs. Following a financial crisis, the board decided this was a weakness demanding correction and now requires unrestricted annual giving by trustees, regardless of their other donations.

It is important to emphasize that many large donors are also active board members and see their donations as part of an overall commitment to the institutions. Moreover, as trustees are socialized into the board and become more knowledgeable, many also assume greater, and more varied, responsibilities. The point of this discussion, accordingly, is not to say that large donors are necessarily uninvolved or that the same individuals cannot contribute wealth, skills, and time. Rather, it is to highlight the fact that finance-related criteria and other governance criteria can, and do, come into tension and lead boards in different directions. It is also to emphasize that these tensions are not coincidental, but rooted in the very nature of these elite boards.

Achieving a Balance: The Case of the Orchid Museum Board

The Orchid Museum board is a case study in both continuity and change. It exemplifies how a traditional upper-class board has evolved in order to maintain an elite institution under changing circumstances. Of the boards studied, that of the Orchid Museum most closely resembles the traditional upper-class board in composition. As we have seen, it has the highest percentage of members who are inheritors, who have the social attributes of elite status (such as club membership, inclusion in bluebooks), and who have longstanding family connections to the institution (chap. 1).

Yet the Orchid Museum board has also changed in many ways as the institution itself has evolved and grown. Indeed, in pursuing organizational growth, the board committed itself to a course of action that required adaptation. To that end, the board incorporated new sources of wealth and types of skills to meet organizational needs. At the same time, it retained both its own stature and that of the institution.

Trustees of varied backgrounds acknowledged and discussed

the board's evolution. As we have already seen, the board incorporated additional sources of funds by becoming more open toward Jews and formerly excluded millionaires (chap. 1). As one
trustee said this gave the museum "support it would not otherwise have gotten." Other types of elites were also recruited for
skills and networks relevant to new and expanded organizational activities. For instance, one CEO, who said, "I can't imag-
ine my being on the board sometime in the past," was recruited
to the board. He was asked to lead a new fundraising effort
in the business community and has served on finance-related
committees. The board also recruited executives with business
expertise specifically relevant to the museum's growing retail
activities. Retail company CEOs, explained one trustee, "gave
us some guidance and insight which we otherwise would not
have had from trustees who served twenty years ago." The board
also supported an aggressive expansion in fundraising activities.
Fundraising campaigns were launched, donation levels needed
to receive various privileges were raised, and advisory bodies
were established to incorporate additional donors.

As the institution grew and became more complex and businesslike, so too did the board. The number of board committees
more than doubled, largely because of the increasing number
and specialization of finance-related committees. One trustee
said, "Increasingly, people are realizing that a large part of this is
just a business." Trustees adapted board recruitment and structure in response to the perceived needs of their expanded and
more complex institution.

Yet the board changed slowly and integrated new members into its prevailing culture and organization. One indication
of the board's approach is found in the evolution of the composition of different board committees. Thus, the "old guard"

continued to dominate the nominating committee and therefore decisions about who would join the board. On the other hand, the finance committees were run by businesspeople lacking in comparable social affiliations. In the early 1970s, the entire nominating committee, and over half of the finance committee were listed in the *Social Register*. By twenty years later, that was still true of all but one member of the nominating committee, but *no* members of the finance committee (or of the separate investment and audit committees created since the earlier period).

The evolution in leadership was also consistent with this picture. On the one hand, all of the current officers were descendants of families with previous ties to the institution. That was also true of over half of the nominating committee. The influential executive committee, however, had diversified considerably, indicating that other types of elite trustees also participate in the board's inner circle. Thus, in the early 1970s, over 85 percent of the executive committee were bluebook listees. Twenty years later, however, this was true of fewer than half of its members. The committee now also included Jewish members, and trustees selected for their business background, as well as descendants of prominent families. As a trustee quoted earlier put it, the "old guard" is still on the board, but now as one group among others. Indeed, changes are ongoing, and since the time of the interviews the nominating committee has come to include its first person of color.

The changes in the board and the organization heighten the businesslike aspects of the board, but these coexist with (rather than supplant) the prestige and class-related elements of board culture. As one trustee put it, "there are not competing elements, there are just different elements." This point is illustrated by a CEO who characterized himself as business oriented and uninterested in the board's "social" dimensions. Yet despite his own outlook, he feels the board should continue to cultivate its social side and recruit individuals who enhance its prestige. In short, the Orchid Museum board has expanded and modified, rather than drastically changed, its culture. In the process, it has only enhanced the institution's stature and affluence.

By way of comparison, it is interesting to consider a different type of change this board made with respect to its composition, namely, the ongoing introduction of members meant to provide wider representation of various parts of Orchid City. These individuals are not expected to be able to provide substantial donative support (although some are also wealthy). These individuals are *not* integrated into the board in the same fashion that we saw above in the case of diversification intended to bring on new elites. Indeed, they never serve for over one term, which typically means that, unless quite wealthy, they are unlikely to have a significant influence. Such individuals themselves believed that this was true, and while some welcomed the opportunity to serve, they also felt that to some extent their inclusion was "window dressing."

Conclusion

Characterizing his elite board, one museum trustee succinctly said, "There's a culture of accumulating money." Trustees of all four of these boards believe that raising funds is a critical trustee responsibility and one that meets institutional needs. The way in which trustees prioritize and approach fundraising is shaped by their elite status and expectations about the elite stature of the institutions. Indeed, the two mutually reinforce one another. Organizational stature enhances trustees' desire to be involved with the organization. Trustees' status provides the organizations with access to a level of resources that not only helps them to function, but to expand and operate as dominant institutions in their field. In the case of museums, this includes not only money but major works of art for the institution's collections.

Trustees characterize their boards as "working" bodies whose members have various responsibilities, and a number of trustees clearly do spend substantial time on governance activities. Yet as trustees recognize, the imperatives of raising money and those of other governance duties do not always coincide. Managing that tension and achieving some type of balance represents one of the major challenges faced by these boards.

Although they say that their boards are active and responsible with respect to governance, trustees' comments reveal their recognition (implicit or explicit) of the tensions and compromises that arise between the board's fundraising priorities and other duties. As we have seen, they acknowledge that some trustees are recruited and kept on the board only because of their financial donations. At the extreme, one board even included a member who was not coherent or able to function. These tensions, and trustees' recognition of them, also emerged when opera trustees compared the opera's board with the board of the opera's support institutions. Repeatedly, they characterized the main opera board as placing more emphasis on wealth, while the support organization boards were described as more hands-on, working bodies, for whom financial ability is less of a priority. These observations were made, moreover, by trustees who served on the boards of both the opera and its support organization. For instance, one said that although many opera trustees "work terribly hard," the board also includes people who are there solely because of their financial resources. By contrast, at the support organization, "they're all expected to take a real responsibility." Similarly, a trustee who serves on the board of the other opera and its support organization said, "The [opera] board is increasingly selecting people who are able to make major financial commitments. The [support organization] board has rich people . . . but they are not there because they're rich. They're there because they can play some role."

An unusual (and less wealthy) trustee in the study, said that, "The board is being used not just as a governing mechanism, but as a way of rewarding big contributors . . . And maybe that's justified, but it does mean that its governance role is diminished." Indeed, he described the board as a "club of very wealthy donors." Although many of his fellow trustees would object that the board does a strong job with respect to its various duties, many would also concur that it includes members whose participation extends little beyond their donations.

Whether or not one agrees with their approach, what is clear is that these boards are deeply shaped by an elite culture and set of expectations concerning the institutions, which require vast resources to sustain. One of the ways that they continue to attract those funds is by creating an exclusive niche for elite participation with the institutions, in which membership on the board is a highly valued form of participation. In doing so, they have created institutions whose stature is even acknowledged by critics. At the same time, however, they continually face the challenge of keeping status and fundraising balanced with the board's oversight mission. For, to return to the trustee quoted at the beginning of this chapter, when the social element goes "out of control" it is the organization that suffers.

Conclusion

This study began by asking whether the class-related meanings and motivations that attract elites to boards also shape how they actually think and behave as trustees. That question has been answered affirmatively, but we have also seen that the influence of class is complex and far from absolute. In particular, we have seen that elite boards must be understood in relation to the dual, and sometimes conflicting, influences of class and organization.

Some have contrasted theoretical approaches according to whether they see formal organizations as instruments of social classes, or view social classes as agents of organizations.[1] Whatever the merits of posing this alternative in other contexts, for the purposes of studying these arts institutions and their boards, such a dichotomy is not applicable. These arts boards are comprised of affluent men and women who infuse class-related values into how they approach organizational governance. Certainly, elites have multiple aesthetic, social, and civic reasons for joining these boards. Yet class serves as a basic framework in which trustees' values, priorities, and motivations are translated into practice.

These operas and museums, however, have evolved into enormous operations that have needs and constraints rooted in their character as large and complex organizations. As one trustee said of his museum, "operationally, it's like a business." Ironically, elites' own pursuit of a costly vision of institutional excellence, which includes a strategy of growth, has contributed to heightening the very organizational influences to which they must adapt. It is an indicator of the strength of their commitment to this vision that they have pursued it even at the cost of diverging at times from traditional patterns of elite exclusivity.

The central thesis of this book has been that, in response to the dual influences of class and organization, elites exhibit a bifurcation in their own approach. When it comes to the institutions and their services, trustees act in ways that are often surprisingly open, adaptive, and that contrast with historical patterns on upper-class boards. Yet when it comes to the board itself, other attitudes and activities perpetuate the board itself as an exclusive and elite enclave. Trustees, in short, function on two distinct but related tracks.

This thesis, as stated at the outset, does not represent a comprehensive explanation of elite boards, which are complex entities that can be illuminated from many points of view. Yet, as we have shown, it does offer a perspective that sheds light on a good deal of board culture and operations across numerous areas, including the seemingly contradictory behavior of boards at times. Moreover, it reveals certain characteristics, dynamics, and tensions that are inherent in the way these boards function and that cut across their individual circumstances and situations. Having reached the conclusion of this analysis, we may now consider some of the additional implications of its perspective.

Arts Participation, Trusteeship, and Elite Exclusivity

A central part of the perspective taken by this book is that, while related, a distinction must be made between an interest in the arts and involvement with the formal organizations that produce and present art. This distinction is consistent with the patterns of exclusivity and openness that trustees display. Elites enjoy and value the arts but do not seek to monopolize the institution's artistic services. Indeed, considerable knowledge of the arts is not even viewed as a requirement for membership on the board.

By contrast, elites do establish and perpetuate an exclusive relationship with the formal organizations that produce art. Charity benefits, privileged access to art exhibitions and special performances, coordinated with dinners and social events, bring elites together in prestigious and exclusive settings. An exhibition opening, remarked one trustee, becomes "a social event, as well as an opportunity to see the art." Black tie events for his museum, another trustee dryly remarked, allow people "to wear their jewelry and their fancy clothes—and then to let everybody know that they could afford to belong to this group." While people join boards for many reasons, membership serves as a way to feel that one is, as a trustee put it, "part of the club."

The way in which elites involve themselves with the arts, accordingly, has social, as well as aesthetic significance. French sociologist Pierre Bourdieu has gone so far as to suggest that the arts play a critical role in elite cohesion.[2] Bourdieu's focus is on distinctive aesthetic orientations and the greater training, familiarity, and ease with high culture he argues exists among elites. In the American context, which we have considered in this book, such cultural familiarity appears to be of lesser importance.[3] Still, the way in which elites participate in the arts, including their philanthropic involvements with arts organizations, does indeed contribute to cohesion among those who participate.[4]

Interestingly, a trustee in this study who is from France, said that, "the overall degree of knowledge of [the American] board is lower than it would be in France. Very broad knowledge of the art field is not one of the requirements." Yet he also observed that board membership is highly coveted and that the financial and social barriers to membership, if not the aesthetic ones, are substantial indeed.

Elite Arts Boards and Arts Policy

These elite arts boards do not exist in a vacuum but are influenced by a wider set of societal decisions and priorities, both implicit and explicit, about support for the arts in the United States. This country has been characterized by an emphasis on private support and governance. Elites were instrumental in creating and sustaining all four of these operas and museums. Without elite support, all of these institutions would be radically different, if they continued to exist at all.

In their position as donors and trustees, elites have not only given financial resources but have shaped the values, mission, and character of these institutions. It is interesting to note that this has been the case even for the two museums, where government has played an important role. Although these museums were founded as a partnership between local government and local elites, from the outset, control was placed in the hands of a private board dominated by the latter.

The system in which these boards function is one that clearly privileges organizations that can attract the support of affluent donors. Within that system, these institutions have done very well indeed. By contrast, institutions that are more distant from the tastes and values of elites will be at a disadvantage in this type of system. Affluent donors have been willing to donate vast sums of money and private collections to organizations that they believe represent the highest levels of artistic excellence. Yet there are other conceptions of the role of art and why and how it should be supported.

For instance, it is unlikely that at least these elites would dedicate comparable resources to innovative and experimental arts organizations. Moreover, today many argue that the value of the arts rests in their connection to communities and strengthening communities. This perspective highlights the contributions of smaller, grassroots institutions that take very different approaches to art and arts participation. Indeed, a trustee in this study, pointedly said that museums should display "art of the ages" and rejected a work of art's connection to a community as a basis for inclusion. Some, however, repudiate precisely that view, characterizing it (and large institutions such as his museum) as embodying an overly Eurocentric and elitist vision of art.[5] Regardless of how one views the value of institutions such as those in this study, the point is that the system in which they have prospered may well fail to provide adequate support for other types of artistic endeavors.

The material presented in this book also indicates that there are boundaries surrounding elite patronage. Trustees, as we have seen, are indeed willing to adapt in order to ensure the health and survival of their institutions. Yet all the evidence suggests that, were the organizations to stray too far from what they consider to be their basic mission, elites would withdraw, or at least reduce, their support. In their eyes, that mission is related to presenting and preserving what they view as the height of artistic excellence. Thus, as one trustee said, while they have various "subplots," such as education, the basic commitment of the board is "to put on the best opera, and be the best opera." It is important to emphasize, moreover, that this comment was made by a trustee who is among those most dedicated to education and outreach activities. Similarly, a trustee of another board said, "I think to go the . . . whole popular route is mistaken. And that's why I also think, that while we have a responsibility in a multiethnic, more urban, society, to respond to the needs of other constituencies, we don't want to get lost."

Status and Governance

As they currently function, elites and institutions engage in a form of exchange.[6] As currently structured, these institutions depend on having access to the resources that can be provided by an elite board. Those resources certainly include money, but they also include valuable art collections and important political and business connections. Yet if elites provide resources for the organizations, the institutions also perform a status-related function for the elite that goes beyond the provision of aesthetic services. Trustees themselves quite consciously cultivate board prestige and exclusivity as a powerful tool in attracting elites and their resources. The evidence presented in this book, moreover, strongly indicates that if the exclusive niche that elites reserve for themselves in relation to these arts institutions were to disappear, elites' financial support would also erode.

From an organizational perspective, however, the danger is that the board's exclusivity and insularity will prevent it from providing adequate leadership in some areas—including some that trustees themselves see as important. Insularity may impede boards from identifying potential problems or responding adequately. External prompting or even crisis may be necessary before boards are willing to change. Elite boards provide organizations with valuable elite connections, but their homogeneity also limits their ability to connect the institutions with other segments of the community. For these reasons, staff's ability to work with the board and the board's receptivity to taking outside help can be crucial.

Furthermore, the danger of the system within which these boards operate is that the status-related dimensions of trusteeship may overwhelm the board's governance functions. It's one thing for trustees to attach class related meanings to boards. It's another thing for them to approach the board as if it were *no more* than a part of their status system. As one trustee put it, when the social element goes "out of control," it's the organization that suffers.

At the same time, it is important to note that, whether or not one agrees, status is an integral and important tool in the way that these boards function. Thus—and again, whether or not one agrees—those who criticize the status-related dimensions of trusteeship must also consider that, from the perspective of institutional support, negative as well as positive consequences could result were they to disappear. Precisely for this reason, the interplay of class and organizational influences is something that researchers, those involved with boards, and boards themselves need to be aware of as these institutions continue to evolve in their shifting environments.

The Complexity of Boards

It is useful to close this book by restating an observation with which it opened, namely, that boards are multifaceted entities that can be studied from multiple perspectives. This book has sought to address and illuminate certain aspects of that complexity, by showing that elite governance must be understood as the joint product of influences rooted both in class values and in the functional needs of formal organizations. In order to understand why and how trustees function as they do, the challenges that these boards face, and their characteristic capabilities and limitations, attention must be given to the overall way in which these two major and fundamental influences come together and operate. In doing so, we are left not only with a fuller picture of underlying factors that shape a wide array of specific trustee actions, but a larger picture of elite boards as cultural, as well as governance, bodies.

NOTES

Introduction

1. Ostrower 1995.
2. According to one figure, cultural institutions in this country rely on private donations for about 40 percent of their revenue (Hodgkinson and Weitzman 1996, p. 12). The comparable figure is far lower in countries such as Britain, Canada, and France (AAFRC 1998, p. 133; Mulcahy 1998). Arts institutions rely more on private donations than do nonprofits over-all, even in the United States (Hodgkinson and Weitzman 1996; Wyszomirski 1989).
3. DiMaggio 1982; DiMaggio and Useem 1982; Jaher 1982; Marcus 1983; Martorella 1982; McCarthy n.d.; Ostrower 1995; Zolberg 1981.
4. Baltzell 1966, pp. 268, 271; Baltzell 1964, pp. 61, 138; see also Domhoff 1974, 1983, p. 17; Useem 1980, pp. 55–56.
5. See discussions of literature by Herman and Van Til 1987; Hall 1999, pp. 33–34.
6. Abzug et al. 1993; Abzug and Galaskiewicz 2001; Ostrower 1995.
7. Pfeffer 1987.
8. For class control perspectives, see Domhoff 1983; Odendahl 1990; Ostrander 1984.
9. So, too, do members of other types of boards (see, e.g., human service agency trustees studied by Widmer 1989).
10. For discussions of prestige as a fundraising tool among elites in other contexts, see Daniels 1988; Galaskiewicz 1985; Ostrower 1995. For a discussion of board reputation in legitimizing nonprofits, see Handy 1995.
11. Ostrower 1995.
12. Among all trustees, 21 percent declined to be interviewed (or, in some cases, initially agreed and then had to cancel, for instance due to their

115

own or a family member's illness). The balance of those not interviewed includes trustees who live far from the city area where interviews were conducted (e.g., in another part of the country), who were traveling during the interview period, for whom information needed to contact them was unavailable, and who were known to be so gravely ill that no attempt to contact them was made. Interviews were conducted between 1993 and 1995.

13. For an extended discussion of role variation within boards, see Widmer 1993.

14. Hodgkinson and Weitzman 1996, p. 244.

15. Abzug et al. 1993; Ostrower 1995; Whitt et al. 1995.

16. Ostrower 1995.

17. The average was 3.5 at both institutions in one city and 3.1 and 2.7 in the other city. The actual percentage of women serving on other boards (90.7 percent) was slightly higher than that of men (81.7 percent), but men with multiple trusteeships had a higher average number of other trusteeships (3.6) than did comparable women (2.4).

18. For instance, in one city over one-third of the trustees from the opera company served on another board with a trustee from the museum. In the other city, that was true for over one-fifth of the opera company trustees. Individuals are also tied to other arts organizations through their spouses. For instance, a very active opera trustee is married to a very active trustee of a modern arts museum in the community, and trustees of one of the operas and museums in this study were married to each other.

19. Women (over 80 percent) were even more likely to sit on another arts board than were men (56.3 percent, $p < .01$). The order of frequency (arts, education, health) was the same among men and women. However, men (21.3 percent) were more likely than women (3.5 percent, $p < .05$) to serve on the board of a nonprofit organization with a policy or economic focus. Among holders of multiple trusteeships, the majority of men (90.6 percent) and women (67.7 percent) sat on a non-arts board, but men were significantly more likely to do so ($p < .01$). This is consistent with other findings (Moore and Whitt 2000) that women who hold multiple trusteeships are more likely to specialize in an area than are men.

20. See Ostrower 1995.

21. Jack Faucett Associates: compiled by Robinson 1993. Survey data show that 3.3 percent of the population reported attending an opera within the previous 12 months. The comparable figure was 26.7 percent

for museums (Jack Faucett Associates: compiled by Robinson 1993, p. 2). See also Netzer 1992.

22. Netzer 1992, p. 186.

23. Baltzell 1964; Pareto 1935.

24. See, for instance, DiMaggio 1982; DiMaggio and Useem 1982; Jaher 1982; McCarthy n.d.; Ostrower 1995, 1998; Whitt et al. 1993; Zolberg 1981.

Chapter One: Elite Trustees: A Profile

1. For instance, among the 164 trustees, gender was identified for 100 percent, information on occupation for over 90 percent, information on assets for 65 percent, and information on income for over half of trustees.

2. Asset data were obtained for 106 trustees. Among cases missing asset data but with income data, over half have incomes in excess of a million dollars a year, indicating that they are also quite wealthy. Income data were available for one-fourth of those missing asset data.

3. The precise percentage of multimillionaires is harder to determine, because of a group of trustees whose assets are only known to fall within a one to five million dollar range, or to exceed a million dollars. A range, however, can be estimated: Under the conservative (and unlikely, since the annual *incomes* of at least some exceed a million dollars) assumption that none in this group are multimillionaires, the multimillionaire category would still include 76 percent of trustees. Conversely, if all of those trustees are assumed to be multimillionaires, the figure rises to 96 percent. Applying this estimating procedure to individual organizations, the *minimum* percentage of multimillionaires ranges from 78 to 89 percent for the Orchid Museum, Tulip Museum, and Orchid Opera boards, and the maximum estimates range from 96 to 100 percent. At the Tulip Opera board, which includes a greater percentage of members in the "low" (1–5 million) asset category, the range is 66 to 94 percent.

4. Percentages for individual boards ranged from a minimum of 35 percent to over 80 percent. Close to 70 percent of trustees had incomes in excess of $500,000. Trustees' affluence is further emphasized when we consider that fewer than 8 percent of all Americans (Hacker 1997), but fully 99 percent of these trustees, had incomes in excess of $100,000 for a comparable year.

5. Percentages ranged from 57 to 82 percent on individual boards.

6. This was true of over 75 percent of businessmen. The balance were

generally other senior officers, such as vice-presidents, and directors of regional corporate offices.

7. See Collins 1988; Daniels 1988; Domhoff 1970; Hacker 1975; McCarthy 1990; Odendahl 1990; Ostrander 1984; Tickamyer 1981.

8. One museum gives ex-officio board status to government representatives, but the other one (although more dependent on government funds) does not, and trustees would oppose their inclusion. Even in the former museum, however, government representatives are not active and do not serve on committees (where central discussions and decisions transpire). Board culture is certainly shaped by its overwhelmingly affluent trustees. Interestingly, while Smith and Lipsky (1993) find that government contracts often pressure social service institutions away from their mission, these elite arts boards felt no pressure or restrictions from government, whose money they feel helps them to pursue their goals for the institution.

9. All of the Hispanic trustees were born and raised outside of the United States, and one resides in another country. Encompassing individuals of varying national origins (e.g., Mexican, Spanish, Puerto Rican), the term "Hispanic" is obviously a broad and diverse category, but the small numbers in this study preclude separate analyses.

10. Of the eleven such trustees, asset levels could be determined for nine, eight of whom proved to be millionaires. Based on what is known about the other two (e.g., their occupation, donations) it is likely that one, but not the other, is a millionaire. Nominating committee members say that they have recruited people with lesser financial resources in order to enhance diversity. As the figures indicate, however, this typically means bringing on those of lesser affluence, not the nonaffluent.

11. The gender composition of nonprofit boards generally, including arts boards, is one on which more data are needed and may well vary considerably among institutions of different types and sizes; see Abzug 1996; Odendahl and Youmans 1994; Slesinger and Moyers 1995, p. 9; Whitt et al. 1993.

12. In 1994, fewer than 7 percent of *Fortune* 1000 directorships were held by women. Forty-two percent had no female members; Zweigenhaft and Domhoff 1998, p. 45, citing Catalyst data.

13. McCarthy 1990. See also Daniels 1988. For the argument that womens' influence on nonprofit boards is strictly circumscribed, see Odendahl and Youmans 1994.

14. Protestants comprised 53 percent of the Orchid City boards, 37

percent of the Tulip Opera board, and just under one third of the Tulip Museum board (the only case in which Protestants, whose numbers were exceeded by Jews, were not the most common religious group). Jews comprised 24–29 percent of the trustees at the first three institutions, and 42 percent of the Tulip Museum board. Just over 10 percent of the Orchid Museum and Tulip Museum, and 20 percent of the Orchid Opera and Tulip Opera trustees were Catholics. The higher percentage of Protestants in Orchid City ($p < .10$) is consistent with its comparatively older and more established elite (differences in the presence of Catholics and Jews were not significant). These figures are based on data for 90 trustees.

15. Interestingly, when trustees were simply asked whether they grew up in an affluent family, the ordering among institutions was precisely the same.

Statistically significant differences in the percentage of inheritors were found between the Orchid Museum and both Tulip City institutions ($p < .05$), and the Orchid and Tulip City Operas ($p = .05$).

16. The low figure at the Tulip Museum, with its high percentage of Jewish members, may reflect the exclusion of Jews from society bluebooks; see Higley 1992.

17. For a list of such schools, see Domhoff 1983. On average, trustees are in their sixties, and many of these schools would have been even more exclusive when they were students.

18. Since the focus is on familial origins, I do not include being preceded on the board by a spouse here.

19. Ostrower 1995. On the increased presence of Jews on boards, see also Abzug and Galaskiewicz 2001; Dain 1991.

20. Lest one suspect that this simply represents a decline in the popularity of the *Register,* it should be noted that every trustee whose parents had been listed was also listed in the *Register.* As this suggests, the lower percentages of listees indicates the greater presence today of board members who are not of "blueblood" origins.

Chapter Two: A Dual Approach: Openness and Exclusivity on the Elite Board

1. See Abzug et al. 1992, p. 290; DiMaggio 1982; DiMaggio and Useem 1982; Jaher 1982; Marcus 1983; Middleton 1987, p. 146; McCarthy n.d.; Ostrower 1995, 1998; Whitt et al. 1993; Zolberg 1981.

2. Ostrower 1995.

3. Figures from one recent year show only 6.9 percent of all giving goes to the combined category of arts, culture, and humanities (AAFRC 1996, p. 13). One economist concludes that "at higher income, giving to . . . cultural institutions becomes much more prominent" (Clotfelter 1992, p. 15).

4. DiMaggio 1982; DiMaggio and Useem 1982; Zolberg 1990, p. 140.

5. DiMaggio 1982; Zolberg 1990.

6. DiMaggio and Useem (1982, p. 190) refer to an orchestra and opera discussed by Arian and Salem, respectively.

7. Smith 1983.

8. See DiMaggio 1982, and DiMaggio and Mohr 1985, who draw on the work of Max Weber.

9. Smith 1983, p. 31.

10. DiMaggio and Useem 1982, p. 190.

Chapter Three: Diversity and the Elite Board: Race, Ethnicity, and Class

1. Baltzell 1964; Pareto 1935.

2. As will be recalled from chapter 1, 90 percent or more of each board's members are whites of non-Hispanic origin, with the balance being comprised of Hispanics and African-Americans.

3. See, for instance, Widmer (1989).

4. Hispanic interviewees used the terms "Hispanic" and "Latino" interchangeably, and that is the usage adopted in this discussion. Unlike "Hispanic-American," moreover, the former terms have the advantage of including both those who are and those who are not American citizens.

5. Indeed, the only cases in which white trustees were critical of the inclusion of a minority trustee or viewed them as "only" on the board because of their minority status were two individuals seen as capable, but unwilling, to make donations (in one case, of any amount at all).

6. One individual did feel quite marginal. Significantly, this trustee (although a millionaire) disliked, and felt ill at ease with, the entire class culture of the board. She attributed her sense of isolation both to this and to a perceived lack of receptivity among board and staff to ideas about enhancing diversity. The other minority member of this board, however, felt quite differently.

7. See Zweigenhaft and Domhoff 1998, who report, for instance, that

under 4 percent of *Fortune* 1000 company directors were black, and fewer than 1 percent each were Asian-American or Hispanic-American. Turning from corporate position to wealth further indicates the lower percentages of minorities within the pool of the economic elite. Thus, in 1995 *Hispanic Business* published a list of the 70 wealthiest Hispanic-Americans. Ten on the list had assets in excess of 100 million dollars, and all had at least 25 million dollars (United Press International, 1 March 1995). By contrast, all 400 of those on *Forbes*'s list of the wealthiest Americans had *minimum* assets in excess of 340 million dollars, which would exclude most on the former list (Forbes, Inc., 1995).

8. Baltzell 1964; Pareto 1935.

Chapter Four: Fundraising and the Role of the Elite Board

1. A majority of every board's trustees (from 63 to 68 percent) cited giving and/or raising money in response to an open-ended question about board functions. Fundraising was the only activity cited by a majority of every board's trustees. It was also the most frequently mentioned, or tied as the most frequently mentioned, function by members of each board.

2. Fully 78 to 94 percent of trustees on each of the boards cited giving and/or fundraising ability as an important criterion.

3. DiMaggio and Useem 1982.

4. Ostrower 1995.

5. Baumol and Bowen (1966) offer a now classic analysis of how the economics of performing arts institutions result in an ever-greater need for subsidies.

6. Of course, trustees and professional staff do not necessarily always agree on what is a worthwhile use of that money. Professional staff, for instance, may be considerably more willing to use funds to subsidize more innovative, but less profitable, programs.

7. The relationships between gender and serving on a development-related committee and serving on a finance-related committee were both statistically significant ($p < .05$).

8. Collins 1992; Daniels 1988; Domhoff 1970; Hacker 1975; McCarthy 1990; Odendahl 1990; Odendahl and Youmans 1994; Ostrower 1995; Ostrander 1984; Tickamyer 1981; Whitt et al. 1993.

9. For a discussion of women's volunteering as an "invisible career," see Daniels 1988.

10. The fourth organization had temporarily disbanded its executive committee, seen as having grown too large to be functional, as part of a board reorganization.

11. For general discussions of changing nonprofit board roles, see Axelrod 1994; Hall 1997, 1999; Wood 1992.

Chapter Five: Status and Governance: A Delicate Balance

1. See also Martorella 1982, p. 41; she observes that patrons and trustees prefer the standard repertoire.

2. Indeed, the Orchid City organizations themselves have taken on a more institutionalized character in the eyes of their trustees, who view them in relation to a long history that they envision as continuing into perpetuity. Tulip City trustees also view their institutions as great and enduring but are closer to their founding and more likely to speak in terms of processes of organizational development.

3. Professional staff, of course, might have provided a different characterization of this situation. What is important for our purposes, however, is that a trustee who disagrees with staff otherwise (whether rightly or wrongly), still defers to them because he believes that their work contributes to organizational excellence.

4. Bowen 1994, p. 43.

5. Similarly, Bowen observes that, "some boards knowingly become larger than they believe they should be because of the high priority given to fund-raising" (1994, p. 44).

Chapter Six: Conclusion

1. See Pfeffer 1987.

2. Bourdieu 1984 (1979).

3. In this respect, the findings reinforce doubts raised by critics of Bourdieu, such as Erickson (1996), Halle (1992), and Lamont (1992) about the importance of extensive, exclusive cultural knowledge as a basis for class solidarity.

4. A more detailed discussion of these points is presented in Ostrower 1998.

5. See Wyszomirski 1995.

6. As Middleton notes, as part of both the organization and its environ-

ment, the board "becomes a resource for each to use" (1987, p. 141; see also Middleton 1989). It is interesting to note, however, that elites themselves consciously "use" their peers as resources to raise money for the institutions they value, a phenomenon characteristic of elite philanthropy more generally (Ostrower 1995).

Abzug, Rikki. 1996. "The Evolution of Trusteeship in the United States: A Roundup of Findings from Six Cities." *Nonprofit Management and Leadership* 7: 101–11.

Abzug, Rikki, and Joseph Galaskiewicz. 2001. "Nonprofit Boards: Crucibles of Expertise or Symbols of Local Identities?" *Nonprofit and Voluntary Sector Quarterly* 30: 51–73.

Abzug, Rikki, Paul J. DiMaggio, Bradford H. Gray, Chul Hee Kang, and Michael Useem. 1993. "Variations in Trusteeship: Cases from Boston and Cleveland, 1925–1985." *Voluntas* 4: 271–300.

American Association of Fund-Raising Counsel. 1998. *Giving USA.* New York: AAFRC Trust for Philanthropy.

American Association of Fund-Raising Counsel. 1996. *Giving USA.* New York: AAFRC Trust for Philanthropy.

Arian, Edward. 1971. *Bach, Beethoven and Bureaucracy: The Case of the Philadelphia Orchestra.* University: University of Alabama Press.

Axelrod, Nancy R. 1994. "Board Leadership and Board Development." In Robert D. Herman and Associates, *The Jossey-Bass Handbook of Nonprofit Leadership and Management,* pp. 119–36. San Francisco: Jossey-Bass Publishers.

Baltzell, E. Digby. 1966 (1953). "*Who's Who in America* and *The Social Register:* Elite and Upper Class Indexes in Metropolitan America." In Reinhard Bendix and Seymour M. Lipset, eds., *Class, Status, and Power: Social Stratification in Comparative Perspective,* pp. 266–71. 2d ed. New York: Free Press.

Baltzell, E. Digby. 1964. *The Protestant Establishment.* New York: Vintage Books.

Baumol, William J., and William G. Bowen. 1966. *Performing Arts: The Economic Dilemma.* Cambridge, Mass.: MIT Press.

Bourdieu, Pierre. 1984 (1979). *Distinction.* Cambridge, Mass.: Harvard University Press.

Bowen, William G. 1994. *Inside the Boardroom: Governance by Directors and Trustees.* New York: John Wiley & Sons.

Clotfelter, Charles T. 1992. "The Distributional Consequences of Non-profit Activities." In Charles T. Clotfelter, ed., *Who Benefits from the Nonprofit Sector?* pp. 1–23. Chicago: University of Chicago Press.

Dain, Phyllis. 1991. "Public Library Governance and a Changing New York City." *Libraries and Culture* 26: 219–50.

Daniels, Arlene K. 1988. *Invisible Careers: Women Civic Leaders from the Volunteer World.* Chicago: University of Chicago Press.

DiMaggio, Paul. 1982. "Cultural Entrepreneurship in Nineteenth-Century Boston, I: The Creation of an Organizational Base for High Culture in America." *Media, Culture, and Society* 4: 33–50.

DiMaggio, Paul, and John Mohr. 1985. "Cultural Capital, Educational Attainment, and Marital Selection." *American Journal of Sociology* 90: 1231–61.

DiMaggio, Paul, and Michael Useem. 1982. "The Arts in Class Repro-duction." In Michael W. Apple, ed., *Cultural and Economic Repro-duction in Education,* pp. 181–201. London: Routledge & Kegan Paul.

Domhoff, G. William. 1983. *Who Rules America Now? A View for the Eighties.* Englewood Cliffs: Prentice-Hall.

Domhoff, G. William. 1974. *The Bohemian Grove and Other Retreats.* New York: Harper & Row.

Erickson, Bonnie H. 1996. "Culture, Class, and Connections." *American Journal of Sociology* 1: 217–51.

Forbes, Inc. 1995. "The 400 Richest People in America." *Forbes,* October 26.

Galaskiewicz, Joseph. 1985. *Social Organization of an Urban Grants Economy.* Orlando, Fla.: Academic Press.

Hacker, Andrew. 1997. *Money: Who Has How Much and Why.* New York: Simon & Schuster.

Hall, Peter Dobkin. 1999. "Resolving the Dilemmas of Democratic Gov-ernance: The Historical Development of Trusteeship in America, 1636–1996." In Ellen Condliffe Lagemann, ed., *Philanthropic Founda-*

tions: New Scholarship, New Possibilities, pp. 3–42. Bloomington: Indiana University Press.

Hall, Peter Dobkin. 1997. *A History of Nonprofit Boards in the United States*. Washington, D.C.: National Center for Nonprofit Boards.

Halle, David. 1992. "The Audience for Abstract Art: Class, Culture, and Power." In Michèle Lamont and Marcel Fournier, eds., *Cultivating Differences: Symbolic Boundaries and the Making of Inequality*, 131–51. Chicago: University of Chicago Press.

Handy, Femida. 1995. "Reputation as Collateral: An Economic Analysis of the Role of Trustees on Nonprofits." *Nonprofit and Voluntary Sector Quarterly* 24: 295–305.

Herman, Robert D. 1989. "Board Functions and Board-Staff Relations in Nonprofit Organizations: An Introduction." In Robert D. Herman and Jon Van Til, eds., *Nonprofit Boards of Directors: Analyses and Applications*, pp. 1–7. New Brunswick, N.J.: Transaction Publishers.

Higley, Stephen Richard. 1992. "The Geography of the *Social Register*." Doctoral diss., University of Illinois at Urbana-Champaign. Distributed by UMI Dissertation Services, Ann Arbor.

Hodgkinson, Virginia A., and Murray S. Weitzman. 1996. *Nonprofit Almanac 1996–1997*. San Francisco: Jossey-Bass Publishers.

Jack Faucett Associates. 1993. *Arts Participation in America: 1982–1992* (compiled by John P. Robinson). Research Division Report #27. Washington, D.C.: National Endowment for the Arts.

Jaher, Frederic Cople. 1982. *The Urban Establishment: Upper Strata in Boston, New York, Charleston, Chicago, and Los Angeles*. Urbana: University of Illinois Press.

Lamont, Michèle. 1992. *Money, Morals, and Manners: The Culture of the French and the American Upper-Middle Class*. Chicago: University of Chicago Press.

Marcus, George. 1983. "Elite Communities and Institutional Orders." In George Marcus, ed., *Elites: Ethnographic Issues*, pp. 41–47. Albuquerque, N.M.: University of New Mexico Press.

Martorella, Rosanne. 1982. *The Sociology of Opera*. New York: Praeger.

McCarthy, Kathleen D. N.D. "Twentieth Century Cultural Patronage." New York: Center for the Study of Philanthropy Working Papers.

McCarthy, Kathleen D. 1990. "Parallel Power Structures: Women and the Voluntary Sphere." In Kathleen D. McCarthy, ed., *Lady Bountiful*

Revisited: Women, Philanthropy, and Power, pp. 1–31. New Brunswick, N.J.: Rutgers University Press.

Middleton, Melissa. 1987. "The Characteristics and Influence of Intraboard Networks: A Case Study of a Nonprofit Board of Directors. In Robert D. Herman and Jon Van Til, eds., *Nonprofit Boards of Directors: Analyses and Applications*, pp. 160–92. New Brunswick, N.J.: Transaction Publishers.

Middleton, Melissa. 1987. "Nonprofit Boards of Directors: Beyond the Governance Function." In Walter W. Powell, ed., *The Nonprofit Sector: A Research Handbook*, pp. 141–53. New Haven: Yale University Press.

Moore, Gwen, and J. Allen Whitt. 2000. "Gender Networks in a Local Voluntary-Sector Elite." *Voluntas* 11: 309–28.

Mulcahy, Kevin V. 1998. "Cultural Patronage in Comparative Perspective: Public Support for the Arts in France, Germany, Norway, and Canada." *Journal of Arts Management, Law, and Society* 27: 247–63.

Netzer, Dick. 1992. "Arts and Culture." In Charles T. Clotfelter, ed., *Who Benefits from the Nonprofit Sector?* pp. 174–206. Chicago: University of Chicago Press.

Odendahl, Teresa. 1990. *Charity Begins at Home: Generosity and Self-Interest among the Philanthropic Elite.* New York: Basic Books.

Odendahl, Teresa, and Sabrina Youmans. 1994. "Women on Nonprofit Boards." In Teresa Odendahl and Michael O'Neill, eds., *Women and Power in the Nonprofit Sector*, pp. 183–221. San Francisco: Jossey-Bass Publishers.

Ostrander, Susan A. 1984. *Women of the Upper Class.* Philadelphia: Temple University Press.

Ostrower, Francie. 1998. "The Arts as Cultural Capital among Elites: Bourdieu's Theory Reconsidered." *Poetics* 26: 43–53.

Ostrower, Francie. 1995. *Why the Wealthy Give.* Princeton: Princeton University Press.

Pareto, Vilfredo. 1935. *Mind and Society*, vol. 3. New York: Harcourt, Brace.

Pfeffer, Jeffrey. 1987. "A Resource Dependence Perspective on Intercorporate Relations." In Mark S. Mizruchi and Michael Schwartz, eds., *Intercorporate Relations: The Structural Analysis of Business*, pp. 25–55. New York: Cambridge University Press.

Salem, Mahmoud. 1984. *Organizational Survival in the Performing Arts: The Making of the Seattle Opera.* New York: Praeger.

Slesinger, Larry H., and Moyers, Richard L. 1995. *A Snapshot of America's*

Nonprofit Boards. Washington, D.C.: National Center for Nonprofit Boards.

Smith, Patrick J. 1983. *A Year at the Met.* New York: Alfred A. Knopf.

Smith, Steven Rathgeb, and Michael Lipsky. 1993. *Nonprofits for Hire: The Welfare State in the Age of Contracting.* Cambridge, Mass.: Harvard University Press.

Tickamyer, Ann R. 1981. "Wealth and Power: A Comparison of Men and Women in the Property Elite." *Social Forces* 60: 463–81.

Useem, Michael. 1980. "Corporations and the Corporate Elite." In Alex Inkeles, Neil J. Smelser, and Ralph Turner, eds., *Annual Review of Sociology,* vol. 6, pp. 41–77. Palo Alto, Calif.: Annual Reviews.

Whitt, J. Allen, Gwen Moore, Cynthia Negrey, Karen King, and Deborah White. 1993. "The Inner Circle of Local Nonprofit Trustees: A Comparison of Attitudes and Backgrounds of Women and Men Board Members." Yale University Program on Non-Profit Organizations Working Paper no. 192. New Haven, Conn.

Widmer, Candace. 1993. "Role Conflict, Role Ambiguity, and Role Overload on Boards of Directors of Nonprofit Human Services Organizations." *Nonprofit and Voluntary Sector Quarterly* 22: 339–56.

Widmer, Candace. 1989. "Why Board Members Participate." In Robert D. Herman and Jon Van Til, eds., *Nonprofit Boards of Directors: Analyses and Applications,* pp. 8–23. New Brunswick, N.J.: Transaction Publishers.

Widmer, Candace. 1989. "Minority Participation on Boards of Directors of Human Service Agencies: Some Evidence and Suggestions." In Robert D. Herman and Jon Van Til, eds., *Nonprofit Boards of Directors: Analyses and Applications,* pp. 139–51. New Brunswick, N.J.: Transaction Publishers.

Wood, Miriam. 1992. "Is Governing Board Behavior Cyclical?" *Nonprofit Management and Leadership* 3: 139–63.

Wyszomirski, Margaret Jane. 1995. "Federal Cultural Support: Toward a New Paradigm?" *Journal of Arts Management, Law, and Society* 25: 69–83.

Wyszomirski, Margaret Jane. 1989. "Sources of Private Support for the Arts: An Overview." In Margaret J. Wyszomirski and Pat Clubb, eds., *The Cost of Culture: Patterns and Prospects of Private Arts Patronage,* pp. 1–8. New York: American Council for the Arts.

Zolberg, Vera L. 1990. *Constructing a Sociology of the Arts.* New York: Cambridge University Press.

Zolberg, Vera L. 1981. "Conflicting Visions in American Art Museums."
    Theory and Society 10: 81–102.
Zweigenhaft, Richard, and Domhof, G. William. 1998. *Diversity in the
    Power Elite: Have Women and Minorities Reached the Top?* New Haven,
    Conn.: Yale University Press.

INDEX

affluence: and arts boards, 3–5, 34, 67; of board members, 3–5, 16, 21, 28, 81; and diversity, 53–57. *See also* class background

African-American board members, 46, 48–52

art collectors, as board members, 7–9, 70, 100, 112

art museums, xxii; and culture of excellence, 87–89; expansion of, 92–93; and government, 9, 118n. 8, 110; social events at, 71; women and, 12, 77

arts administrators, xiv, 19, 64; autonomy of, 94, 122n. 3; and culture of excellence, 93–95; fundraising by, 69, 72, 121n. 6; goals of, 88–89

arts boards: and affluence, 3–5, 34, 67; and arts administrators, 93–95; changes in, 18–23, 101–4; composition of, 1–23; conservatism of, 18, 88–89, 111; culture of, 4, 85–89; diversity of, 2, 18, 20, 39–42, 57–62, 104; as exclusive, 33–35, 37–38, 85–86, 106, 112; and fundraising, 63–66, 92, 97–98, 104; and governance, 85, 95–101, 105–6, 113; homogeneity of, 58–62, 112–13; influences on, xvi; and prestige, xvi, 33–35, 97; publicized, 2–3; significance of, xiii–xvi; size of, 96–97; and social events, 34–35, 109. *See also* board members

arts institutions: annual reports of, 30; as businesses, 22, 37, 79–80; commercial activities of, 7, 22, 31–33, 36–37, 79; and civic stature, 89–91; diverse audiences of, 40–41, 50, 54–57; donations to, xviii; educational activities of, 82–83, 111; exclusivity of, 29–30; expansion of, 92–93; experimental, 111; finance of, 7; government support of, 10, 80, 110; income of, 69; interest in, of elites, xiv, xviii, 25–27, 108–10; missions of, 25–26, 111; openness of, 24–25; policies of, 110–12; prestige of, 27–29, 33–35, 69, 72–74, 87–89; private support of, xiii, 110, 115n. 2; staff of (*see* arts administrators). *See also* art museums; opera companies

audiences, of arts institutions: diversity of, 40–41; and inclusiveness, 111–12

bifurcation. *See* duality

board members: affluence of, 3–5, 16, 21, 28, 34, 81; African-American, 46, 48–52; art collecting by, 7–9, 70, 100, 112; business background of, 48, 50–51, 80, 82, 99, 102–3; class background of, xvi, 2, 39–40, 68–72, 82, 101; and club membership, xxi, 4, 101; controversial nominations of, 17; donations by, 5, 66–68, 70, 79, 86–87, 97–98; duality in outlook of,

board members (*continued*)
xvi–xvii, 24–25, 63; education of, 14; ethnic identity of, 45–52; European, 26; families of, 13–15; financial management by, 7, 73, 77–79, 102; fundraising by, 63–66, 78–84; gender of, 2, 5–7, 11–12, 74–78, 116n. 17; Hispanic, 44–45, 48–52, 56–57, 118n. 9; honorary, 97–98; interest in art of, xviii, 25–27, 108–10; Jewish, 13, 18–19, 21, 68, 102–3; occupations of, 5–7; political connections of, 9–10; race of, 2, 11, 48–52; recruitment of, 1–2, 12, 15–18, 40, 53–57; religion of, 12–13, 18–19, 118–19n. 14; roles of, 66, 78–82; and social service, xxi; status of, 69, 72, 85, 113; turnover of, 12, 99–100. *See also* arts boards
Bourdieu, Pierre, 109
business: arts institutions as, 22, 37, 79–80; and board membership, 48, 50–51, 80, 82, 102; women in, 6, 76–78. *See also* marketing

change, in arts boards, 18–23, 101–4; and demographic change, 43–44; and elite status, xxiii, 30, 39, 57; and social change, 42; turnover of board members, 12, 99–100; and urban environments, xxiv. *See also* class background; diversity; gender
civic stature, and arts institutions, 89–91
class background: of African-American board members, 48–52; of board members, xvi, 2, 39–40; and diversity, 45–47, 53–57; and fundraising, 68–74, 82; of Hispanic board members, 48–52; and organizations, 107–8; and perspective, xvii–xix. *See also* affluence
corporate boards, compared to nonprofits, 67

DiMaggio, Paul, 20, 29
diversity: and affluence, 53–57; of arts boards, 2, 18, 20, 39–42, 57–62; and audiences of arts institutions, 40–41; and class background, 45–47, 53–57; and demographic changes, 43–44; and duality, 40–42; and social changes, 42
Domhoff, G. William, 15
duality, in outlook of arts boards, xvi–xvii, 24–25, 29–30, 33–35, 63, 108; and artistic mission, 25–27; and diversity, 40–42; and fundraising, 64–65; and minority trustees, 49–52; and needs of arts institutions, 35–38, 42–45, 85; and prestige of arts institutions, 27–29. *See also* change; exclusivity; openness

education: of board members, 14; as mission of arts institutions, 82–83
elite status: and adaptation, xxiii, 30, 39, 57; and art collecting, 7–9; of arts institutions, 109; and board membership, xii–xiii, 25, 101, 106; defined, xi–xii; and family, xiv, 13–15; and fundraising, 63–64; and organizations, xv; and political connections, 9–10. *See also* exclusivity; prestige
ethnic identity, of board members, 45–52. *See also* race
excellence, culture of: on arts boards, 85–89; and fundraising, 95–101; and growth of arts institutions, 92–93
exclusivity: of arts boards, 33–35, 37–38, 85–86, 106, 112; of arts institutions, 29–31; and diversity, 45–47; and fundraising, 64, 68. *See also* elite status; prestige

family, of board members, xiv, 13–15
financial management, of arts institutions, 7, 73, 77–78
Forbes, 3
Fortune, 118n. 12
fundraising: and affluence, 67–68; by arts administrators, 69, 72; and class background, 68–74, 82; by board members, 63–66, 78–84, 104; and culture of excellence, 95–101; and elite status, 63–64; and exclusivity,

64, 68; and gender, 65, 74–78; and governance, 95–101; as mission of arts boards, 66–68; social events for, 70–71, 73. *See also* business; financial management; marketing

gender: of board members, 2, 11–12, 116n. 17; and fundraising, 65; influence on trustee roles of, 74–78; and occupation of board members, 5–7. *See also* women
governance, of arts institutions, 85, 95–101, 104–5
government funding: of art museums, 9, 78; of arts institutions, 10, 80

Hispanic audiences, of opera, 44, 54–57
Hispanic board members, 44–45, 48–52, 56–57, 118n. 9

Jewish board members, 13, 18–19, 21, 68, 102–3

marketing, of arts institutions, 7, 22, 31–33

nonprofit boards, xv, 63–64, 67, 69, 115n. 2, 118n. 11. *See also* arts boards

openness, of arts boards: and audience expansion, 30–31; and marketing, 31–33; and needs of arts institutions, 35–38. *See also* change; diversity
opera companies, xxii; and affluence, 4; audiences of, 30–31; boards of, 25–26, 105–6; commercial activities of, 36; and culture of excellence, 87–89; as elitist, 29; expansion of, 92–93; fundraising by, 69, 73; and Hispanic audiences, 44, 54–55; prestige of, 27; repertory of, 30; and social events, 73–74; and supertitles, 30–31

philanthropy, xii; and civic stature, 91; and class background, 47; and culture, 29; in New York, 28; patterns in, xxi–xxii; and women, 11. *See also* fundraising
prestige: and arts boards, xvi, 33–35, 97; of arts institutions, 27–29, 33–35, 69, 72–74, 87–89; of cities, 89–91; of opera, 27. *See also* elite status; exclusivity

race: and affluence, 45–47; of board members, 2, 11
recruitment, of board members, 1–2, 12, 15–18; and diversity, 40, 53–57, 60–62
religion: of board members, 12–13, 18–19, 118–19n. 14

Smith, Patrick J., 29
social events: of arts boards, 34–35; and fundraising, 70–71, 73; and opera, 73–74; women as organizers of, 75–78
Social Register, 21, 103, 119n. 20
society bluebooks, 13, 101, 103
supertitles, at opera performances, 30–31

trustees. *See* board members

urban environments, changes in, xxiv
Useem, Michael, 20, 29

Who's Who, 3
women: and art museums, 77; in business, 6, 11, 76–78; class background of, 74; and philanthropy, 11–12; and social events, 75–78. *See also* gender